Janice VanCleave's

A+
PROJECTS IN
BIOLOGY

Winning Experiments for
Science Fairs and Extra Credit

John Wiley & Sons, Inc.

NEW YORK · CHICHESTER · BRISBANE · TORONTO · SINGAPORE

Copyright © 1993 by John Wiley & Sons, Inc.

Library of Congress Cataloging-in-Publication Data

VanCleave, Janice Pratt.
    [A+ projects in biology]
    Janice VanCleave's A+ projects in biology : winning experiments
for science fairs and extra credit.
        p.   cm.
    Includes index.
    Summary: A collection of experiments and projects exploring
various aspects of biology.
    ISBN 0-471-58629-3 (cloth).—ISBN 0-471-58628-5 (pbk.)
    1. Biology projects—Juvenile literature.   2. Human biology—
Experiments—Juvenile literature.   [1. Science projects.
2. Experiments.]   I. Title.   II. Title: A+ projects in biology.
III. Title: Janice VanCleave's A-plus projects in biology.
QH316.5.V35 1993
574'.078—dc20
93-13306

Printed in the United States of America
10   9

This book is dedicated to two very special
people in my life:

Kate Bradford and Fred Nachbaur

Contents

Introduction

Science is a search for answers to all kinds of interesting questions about our world. Science projects make excellent tools for you to use as you look for the answers to specific problems. This book will give you guidance and provide A+ project ideas. An A+ idea is not a guarantee that you will receive an A+ grade on your project. Your grade will depend on you. You must do your part by planning experiments, finding and recording information related to a problem, and organizing the data to find its answer.

Sharing your findings by presenting your project at science fairs will be a rewarding experience if you have properly prepared the exhibit. Trying to assemble a project overnight usually results in frustration, and you cheat yourself out of the fun of being a science detective. Solving a scientific mystery, like solving a detective mystery, requires that you plan well and carefully collect facts.

Start your project with curiosity and a desire to learn something new. Then, proceed with a purpose and a determination to solve the problem. It is likely that your scientific quest will end with some interesting answers.

Select a Topic

The 30 topics in this book suggest many possible problems to solve. Each topic has one "cookbook" experiment—follow the recipe, and the result is guaranteed. Read all of these easy experiments before choosing the topic you like best and want to know more about. Regardless of the problem you choose to solve, your discoveries will make you more knowledgeable about biology.

Each of the 30 sample projects begins with a brief summary of topics to be studied and objectives to be determined. Information relevant to the project is also included in the opening summary. Terms are defined when first used, but definitions are not repeated throughout the text. Check the Glossary and/or Index to find explanations about any terms that are unfamiliar to you.

Try New Approaches

Following each of the 30 introductory experiments is a section titled "Try New Approaches" that provides additional questions about the problem presented. By making small changes to some part of the sample experiment, new results are achieved. Think about why these new results might have happened.

Design Your Own Experiment

In each chapter, the section titled "Design Your Own Experiment" allows you to create experiments to solve the questions asked in "Try New Approaches." Your own experiment should follow the sample experiment's format and include a single purpose or statement; a list of necessary materials; a detailed step-by-step procedure; written results with diagrams, graphs, and charts, if they seem helpful; and a conclusion explaining why you got the results you did and answering the question you posed to yourself. To clarify your answer, include any information you found through research. When you design your own experiment, make sure to get adult approval if supplies or procedures other than those given in this book are used.

Get the Facts

Read about your topic in many books and magazines. You are more likely to have a successful project if you are well informed about the topic. For each topic in this book, the section titled "Get the Facts" provides some tips to guide you to specific sources of information. Keep a journal to record all the information you find from each source including the author's name, the title of the book or article, the numbers of the pages you read, the publisher's name, the city of publication, and the year of publication.

Keep a Journal

Purchase a bound notebook to serve as your journal. Write in it everything relating to the project. It should contain your original ideas as well as ideas you get from books or from people like teachers and scientists. It should also include descriptions of your experiments as well as diagrams, photographs, and written observations of all your results.

Every entry should be as neat as possible and dated. A neat, orderly journal provides a complete and accurate record of your project from start to finish and can be used to write your project report. It is also proof of the time you spent sleuthing out the answers to the scientific mystery you undertook to solve, and you will want to display the journal with your completed project.

Use the Scientific Method

Each project idea in this book will provide foundation material to guide you in planning what could be a prize-winning project. With your topic in mind and some background information, you are ready to demonstrate a scientific principle or to solve a scientific problem via the **scientific method**. This method of scientifically finding answers involves the following steps: purpose, hypothesis, research, experimentation, and conclusion. Each step is described next.

Research: The process of collecting information about the topic being studied. It is listed as a first step because some research must be done first to formulate the purpose and hypothesis and then to explain experimental results.

Purpose: A statement that expresses the problem or question for which you are seeking resolution. You must have some knowledge about a topic before you can formulate a question that can lead to problem-solving experimentation. Thus, some research is necessary for this step, and you can find much of the information about each topic in this book.

Hypothesis: A guess about the answer to the problem based on knowledge and research you have before beginning the project. It is most important to write down your hypothesis before beginning the project and not to change it even if experimentation proves you wrong.

Experimentation: The process of testing your hypothesis. Safety is of utmost importance. The projects in this book are designed to encourage you to learn more about a biological phenomenon by altering a known procedure, but only with adult supervision should you explore untested procedures.

Conclusion: A summary of the experimental results and a statement that addresses how the results relate to the purpose of the experiment. Reasons for experimental results that are contrary to the hypothesis are included.

Assemble the Display

Keep in mind that while your display respresents all that you have done, it must tell the story of the project in such a way that it attracts and holds

Figure I.1

the viewer's interest. So, keep it simple. Try not to cram all your information into one place. To conserve space on the display, and still exhibit all your work, keep some of the charts, graphs, pictures, and other materials in your journal instead of on the display board itself.

The actual size and shape of displays vary according to local science fair official rules. So, remember to check them out for your particular fair. Most exhibits are allowed to be 48 inches (122 cm) wide, 30 inches (76 cm) deep, and 108 inches (274 cm) high. Your display may be smaller than these maximum measurements. A three-sided backboard (see Figure I.1) is usually the best way to display your work. Wooden panels can be hinged together, but you can also use sturdy cardboard pieces taped together to form a very inexpensive, but presentable, exhibit.

A good title of eight words or less should be placed at the top of the center panel. The title should capture the theme of the project but not be the same as the problem statement. For example, suppose the problem under question is, Are dishwashing sponges vehicles conducive to the growth of bacteria? An effective title might be, *Dishwashing Sponges: A Bacteria Culture.* The title and other headings should be neat and also large enough to be readable from a distance of about 3 feet (1 m). You can glue letters onto the backboard (buy precut letters or cut some out of construction paper), or you can stencil them for all the titles. A short summary paragraph of about 100 words to explain the scientific principles involved is useful and can be printed under the title. Someone who has no knowledge of the topic should be able to easily understand the basic idea of the project just by reading the summary.

There are no set rules about the position of the information on the display. However, it all needs to be well organized, with the title and summary paragraph as the focal point at the top of the center panel and the remaining material placed neatly from left to right under specific headings. The headings you display will depend on how you wish to organize the information. Separate headings of "Problem," "Procedure," "Results," and "Conclusion" may be used.

Discuss the Project

The judges give points for how clearly you are able to discuss the project and explain its purpose, procedure, results, and conclusion. While the display should be organized so that it explains everything, your ability to discuss your project and answer the questions of the judges convinces them that you did the work and understand what you have done. Practice a speech in front of friends, and invite them to ask you questions. If you do not know the answer to a question, never guess or make up an answer or just say, "I do not know." Instead, say that you did not discover that answer during your research, and then offer other information that you found of interest about the project. Be proud of the project, and approach the judges with enthusiasm about your work.

PART I

Botany

1 | Seed Parts: Exterior and Interior

Given the right amount of water, oxygen, and warmth, most seeds germinate and develop into mature plants. Seeds vary in physical appearance both on the outside and on the inside.

In this project, you will have the opportunity to identify exterior and interior seed parts. The seed parts of two basic seed types, dicotyledons and monocotyledons, will be compared. You will determine why the cotyledon is necessary and investigate the presence of starch in each seed part.

Getting Started

Purpose: To dissect a bean seed and identify its parts.

Materials

8 to 10 pinto beans	paper towel
1-pint (500-ml) jar	magnifying lens (handheld type)
distilled water	
refrigerator	

Procedure

1. Place the beans into the jar and cover them with distilled water.
2. Put the jar of beans in the refrigerator to reduce bacterial contamination.
3. Soak the beans for 24 hours.
4. Remove the beans from the jar and place them on the paper towel to absorb the excess water.
5. Inspect the outside of the beans and identify the seed coat, micropyle, and hilum (see Figure 1.1).
6. Use your fingernails to carefully remove the seed coat from one of the beans.
7. Very gently pry the rounded side of the bean open like a book with your fingernail.

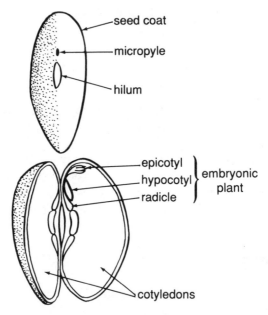

Figure 1.1

8. Spread open the two halves of the bean.

9. Use the magnifying lens to study the inside of each bean half and identify the cotyledon, epicotyl, hypocotyl, and radicle (see Figure 1.1).

10. Open several beans and compare their parts for differences in size, shape, and organization.

Results

The brown seed coat is thin and peels off easily to reveal a white structure with two separate halves connected at the top. Inside is a cylindrical structure with what appears to be folded leaves at the end.

Why?

The bean seed consists of three parts: a seed coat, an embryo, and two **cotyledons** (food-storage tissue). The surface covering of a seed is called the **seed coat.** This jacket around the seed protects the **embryo** (baby plant inside the seed) from insects, disease, and damage. The scar on the seed coat is the **hilum** (point of attachment to the ovary wall). The small dot at one end of the hilum is the **micropyle** (small opening through which pollen grains enter).

The bean is a **dicotyledon** because it has *two* bean halves under the seed coat. Inside the cotyledons is the embryo, the cylindrical structure within the seed that **germinates** (develops into a plant). The lower end of the peg-shaped **hypocotyl** which develops into the plant's first root is called the **radicle.** The section of the **hypocotyl** above the radicle becomes the plant's lower stem. The **epicotyl** on the end, which looks like folded leaves, forms the plant's first true leaves.

Try New Approaches

1a. While dicotyledons have two seed leaves, **monocotyledons** have only *one* seed leaf. How do the seed parts of a monocotyledon compare to those of a dicotyledon? Repeat the experiment replacing the bean seed with corn seed. Corn seed is much more difficult to open and may require the use of a single-edge razor blade. As in the original experiment, study and identify seed parts (see the corn seed diagram in Figure 1.2).

CAUTION: Always be careful when cutting with a sharp instrument to cut in a direction away from your hands and fingers.

   b. Use a **stereomicroscope** (dissecting microscope that allows thick specimens to be observed) to study, identify, and compare the parts of bean seed and corn seed. **Science Fair Hint:** Diagram the parts of each seed type, label the parts, and display the diagrams.

   2. How much of the cotyledon is necessary for development of the embryo? Soak 20 beans for 24 hours in a jar of water. Prepare four beans for each of the following five sections:
   - 100%—Do not cut away any part of the cotyledons.
   - 75%—Cut away the lower half of one cotyledon.
   - 50%—Cut away the lower half of both cotyledons.
   - 25%—Cut away all but one-fourth of the cotyledons, leaving the section attached to the embryo.
   - 0%—Cut away both cotyledons, leaving only the embryo.

   Note: Use a single-edge razor blade to carefully cut away the indicated parts of the cotyledons (see Figure 1.3). Make every effort not to disturb the embryo. Discard extra beans.

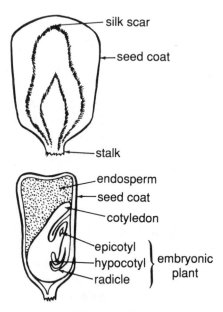

Figure 1.2

Place the prepared beans on a moist paper towel. Set the towel on a sheet of aluminum foil and fold the foil around the beans. Open the foil package daily and make observations of any evidence of germination. **Science Fair Hint:** Use diagrams and photographs to represent results.

Design Your Own Experiment

1. Starch is a stored food supply for seeds. Is starch stored in seed parts other than the cotyledons? Using beans and corn seeds, determine the presence of starch by using iodine on each of the following seed parts: cotyledon, endosperm, epicotyl, hypocotyl, radicle, and seed coat. Separate the parts from one another and place them in shallow containers. Add one or two drops of tincture of iodine (found at a pharmacy) to each part. **CAUTION:** Keep the iodine out of reach of small children. It is poisonous and is for external use only. A color of blue to blue-black indicates that starch is present in the material that the iodine touches. Prepare and display a data table to indicate the presence of starch. Use a plus sign (+) to indicate the presence of starch and a minus sign (−) to indicate its absence.

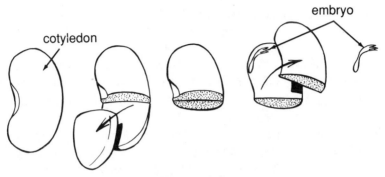

Figure 1.3

2. Seeds vary in size, shape, and color. Collect and display samples of seeds. Organize the seeds to indicate which are **angiosperms** (flowering plants) and which are **gymnosperms** (evergreens or conifers). Further classifications, such as how the seeds are transported, can also be used.

Get the Facts

1. *Endosperm* (the food-storage tissue of a seed) is present at some stage during the development of all seeds. It is present in mature corn seed but not in bean seed. What happens to the endosperm? Why is it present in some mature seeds but not in others?

2. Some plants, such as milkweed, have a parachutelike structure attached to each seed so that it will float easily and be carried by even the lightest wind. Find out more about seed dispersal, which is the way that seeds are carried by wind, water, and animals.

3. The most abundant plants are those that reproduce by seeds. Find out about the reproductive cycle of seed-bearing plants. How does seed production differ between the two classes of seed-bearing plants (angiosperms and gymnosperms)? Diagram the reproductive cycle of different seed-bearing plants.

4. The seed coat of different seeds varies in color, thickness, and texture. Sometimes, it is smooth and paper-thin, as on a bean. A coconut's seed coat is rough, thick, and hard. This outer coat protects the embryo from drying out, against injury from falls or being struck by objects, and from attacks by insects, bacteria, and fungi. It also insulates the embryo from extreme temperatures. Germination cannot take place

unless the seed coat is cracked. The seed coats of some plants are cracked by alternate freezing and thawing. Not all seeds are affected by temperature changes, and many plants do not live where the temperature drastically rises and falls. How else might a seed coat crack, allowing water and oxygen in and the developing embryo to emerge?

5. Many types of seeds do not germinate regardless of the environmental conditions. They germinate only after a period of rest called the *dormancy period*. Dormancy may be the result of many factors; for example, the seed coat may contain chemical inhibitors that prevent germination. During a period of rest, soil moisture leaches out the chemicals or they break down as they react with other chemicals in the soil. When the inhibitors are gone, the seed germinates. Find out more about seed dormancy and the events that result during a rest period.

Necessary Nutrients for Seed Germination

2

Plants rooted in soil obtain nourishment from it. Soil supplies nitrogen, phosphorus, potassium, and other chemical nutrients for plant growth and development.

In this project, you will determine whether nutrients in the soil are necessary for seed germination. You will find the answer to the question, Can plants develop with only the nutrients provided by the soil? You will also compare seedlings grown in commercial liquid fertilizers to those grown in nutrients leached from soil.

Getting Started

Purpose: To determine whether added nutrients speed up seed germination.

Materials

10 pinto beans	marking pen
1-pint (500-ml) jar	masking tape
distilled water	paper towels
refrigerator	2 straight-sided drinking glasses
liquid plant fertilizer (5–10–5)	
1-gallon (4-liter) plastic milk jug	2 sheets of black construction paper
	stapler

Procedure

1. Place the beans into the jar and cover them with distilled water.

2. Put the jar of beans in the refrigerator to soak overnight.

3. Prepare 1 gallon (4 liters) of the commercial liquid plant fertilizer by following the instructions on the package. Use distilled water to mix the fertilizer in the milk jug.

Figure 2.1

4. With the marking pen, write "Nutrients" on a piece of masking tape and tape this label to the jug of liquid fertilizer.

5. Prepare two separate containers of beans as follows:

   a. Fold one paper towel and line the inside of a glass with it.

   b. Wad together several paper towels and stuff them into the glass to hold the paper lining against the glass.

   c. Place five beans between the glass and the paper towel lining, evenly spacing the beans around the perimeter of the glass.

6. Use the marking pen and tape to label one glass "Water" and the second glass "Nutrients" (see Figure 2.1).

7. Moisten the paper towel in each glass with either distilled water or plant fertilizer as indicated. Keep the paper towels in the glasses moist, but not dripping wet, during the entire experiment.

8. Cover the outside of each glass with one sheet of black construction paper. Fold and staple the top and sides of the paper.

9. Each day, until each bean germinates (five to seven days), remove the paper covering from each glass and observe the contents (see Figure 2.2).

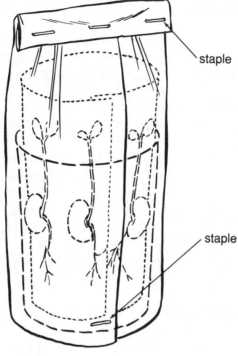

staple

staple

Figure 2.2

Results

The beans in each glass may vary somewhat in the time required for germination, but there is no major difference in the germination time of the beans with and without added nutrients.

Why?

The bean seeds moistened by water and those moistened by a **nutrient** (nourishment or food that promotes growth in living organisms) show no difference in the rate of their germination. Germination occurs even when there is a lack of nitrogen, phosphorus, potassium, and other nutrients. The nutrients in the soil are not used by the bean seeds to germinate. The seeds germinate (develop from a seed into a plant) when the content of each seed has properly matured and when the amounts of oxygen and moisture are adequate and the temperature is correct. The food supply necessary for germination is stored in the cotyledons (seed leaves) of the bean.

Try New Approaches

1. How long does a bean plant grow with food supplied only from the cotyledons? Continue to water the contents of each glass with the indicated liquid. *Note:* Keep the glasses and plants covered with dark paper so that the plants do not receive light and produce food by **photosynthesis** (the formation of carbohydrates in chlorophyll-containing tissue of plants exposed to light). Measure and record the daily growth and development of each bean seedling. Continue observations for 30 days or until one or both sets of plants die.

2. Does the growing medium affect the results? The paper towel provides no nutrients to the growing plant. Repeat the original experiment using other nonnutrient mediums such as LECA (light expanded clay aggregate), sand, gravel, charcoal, sawdust, and vermiculite or perlite.

3a. Can seedlings mature with only the food produced in their leaves by the reaction of photosynthesis? Repeat the original experiment omitting the black paper covering and instead placing the glasses where they will receive equal amounts of sunlight each day. Measure and record the daily growth and development of leaves, stems, and roots. Continue observations for 30 days or until one or both sets of plants die.

b. Make your own plant fertilizer and compare its results with the purchased commercial fertilizer. Growing plants in liquid nutrients without soil is called **hydroponics.** A homemade hydroponic solution can be made by mixing together 1 teaspoon (5 ml) each of baking soda and Epsom salt and 1 tablespoon (15 ml) each of saltpeter (sodium nitrate) and household ammonia. Mix in 1 gallon (4 liters) of tap water that has been allowed to stand in an open container for one day so that the chlorine added by municipal water suppliers can evaporate. Do not use water that has been processed by a water conditioner. Hard water is actually better than soft water because it contains calcium and magnesium, which are useful to plants. Repeat the previous experiment using the commercial nutrient to water one container and the homemade nutrient to water the second container. Make daily observations and determine how long the plants survive with artifically added nutrients.

c. Plants in nature do not receive commercial or homemade fertilizers. Repeat the original experiment using nutrients from soil. Remove the

nutrients from soil by filtering water through nutrient-rich soil se-
cured from a nursery or a wooded area. Put the soil in a cheesecloth
and set the cloth in a food colander that rests on the rim of a large
pot. Pour 1 gallon (4 liters) of water into the soil. After all of the water
has drained through, remove the water from the pot and pour it into
the soil again. Repeat this procedure six times so that the water dis-
solves as many of the nutrients in the soil as possible.

Design Your Own Experiment

1. Do all soils provide the necessary nutrients for plant growth? Collect
   soil samples from as many different locations as possible. Prepare containers for the different soil samples and plant seed such as ryegrass
   seed in each container. Make a data table for each seed used similar
   to the one for rye grass seed shown here to record observations from
   each experiment. Keep all tables in your journal. To represent the
   progress of the experiments, display the data tables along with photographs taken of the developmental stages of the plants.

2. Do different types of grass give the same results in the soil as the
   ryegrass seed? Repeat the previous experiment using the same soil
   samples but different grass seed. Use photographs and diagrams
   showing the development of the plants to represent the procedure and
   results. Display living plants. Remember to plant seeds the appropriate
   number of days before the science fair in order to have samples ready
   for the project display.

Data Growth Table for Rye Seed		
	Soil		
	Sample 1	Sample 2	Sample 3
Day 1			

Get the Facts

1. All commercial fertilizers are labeled with numbers to give the buyer
   information about the nutrient content of the products. Each product
   may have a different amount of each nutrient, but the listings are al-

ways in the same order. Use a gardening book to find information about this labeling code. What are the identified nutrients and what is their order in the number code? What does it mean when the fertilizer is labeled 5–10–5?

2. Fertilizers can provide necessary nutrients for plant growth. Is it always necessary to use these additives? Can they be overused? Runoff water contains dissolved materials from the soil. How do fertilizers washed out of the soil affect living organisms in rivers, lakes, streams, or other bodies of water? The United States Agricultural Extension Service has an office in every county seat. This agency can provide information about fertilizers and their uses and safety.

3. Some gardeners use *organic* nutrients. Find out more about organic gardening. How do organic nutrients affect the environment? What is a *compost*? Can organic nutrients be used for large-scale food production?

3 Nutrient Differences in Soils

Plants grow in natural environments without the assistance of commercial fertilizers. The soil seems to provide all the nutrients the plants need. Is there a difference in the nutrients in soils from one location to another?

In this project, you will test the effects on plant growth of nutrients leached from soil samples taken from different environments. You will also discover which nutrients are best for plants.

Getting Started

Purpose: To determine whether nutrients leached from potting soil are sufficient for plant growth.

Materials

5-gallon (20-liter) bucket or container

water

2-quart (2-liter) food colander

4 2-gallon (8-liter) cooking pots with openings large enough to support the colander

2 2-×-2-foot (60-×-60-cm) pieces of cheesecloth

2 quarts (2 liters) of potting soil

1-quart (1-liter) jar

funnel

4 1-gallon (4-liter) plastic milk jugs with caps

marking pen

masking tape

4 houseplants (same kind and size and each with five or more leaves)

sand

Procedure

1. Fill the bucket with tap water. Allow the water to stand in this open container for one day so that the chlorine in the water can evaporate. *Note:* Use this water when water is requested in the procedure.

2. Place the food colander over the opening in one pot so that the rim of the pot supports the colander.

3. Line the inside of the colander with one piece of cheesecloth.

4. Fill the cloth-lined colander with potting soil.

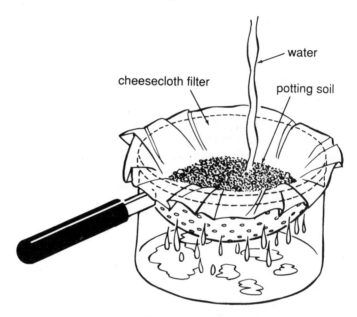

Figure 3.1

5. Use the jar to pour 2 gallons (8 liters) of water into the soil (see Figure 3.1). *Note:* It will take time for all of the water to drain through the soil, so add the water slowly. The water draining through the soil is called the **filtrate.**

6. After all of the filtrate has drained through the soil, lift the soil-filled colander and place it over one of the empty pots.

7. Pour the filtrate into the soil again.

8. Repeat this procedure (steps 6 and 7) three times.

9. Use the funnel to pour the nutrient-rich filtrate into two empty milk jugs. Cap the jugs.

10. With the marking pen, write "Nutrient Filtrate" on pieces of masking tape and tape these labels to the jugs.

11. Discard the soil. Wash the colander with tap water and place it over one clean pot.

12. Line the colander with the second (clean) piece of cheesecloth.

13. Pour water through the cloth. After all the water has drained through the cloth, lift the colander and place it over another clean pot. Pour the water from the first pot through the colander. Repeat six times before pouring it into the two empty milk jugs. You want to control any difference in impurities picked up by the water as it passes through the cloth.

14. Label the jugs "Water Only." Cap the jugs.

15. Remove the plants from their containers. Gently shake the soil from their roots and stand the plants in the bucket of water.

16. Remove all the soil from the plant containers, rinse them with tap water, and repot the plants using sand instead of soil.

17. Use the marking pen and tape to label two of the containers "Water Only" and the remaining two "Nutrient Filtrate."

18. Place the plants together so that their environment (temperature, amount of sunlight, and so on) is the same.

19. Keep the sand moist, but not dripping wet, using the appropriate liquid. Add the same amount of liquid to each plant.

20. Observe and record the growth of the plants for four weeks.

Results

The results may vary, but the author found that the nutrient-fed plants had stronger stems and greener leaves.

Why?

Many chemicals needed for plant growth are soluble in water. Because of their solubility, as the water passes through the soil, these chemicals dissolve in the water and pass through the holes in the cheesecloth. The process of removing these soluble chemicals is called **leaching.** The filtrate collected by leaching is rich in nutrients needed for plant growth. Plants grown with this nutrient liquid grow better than plants grown without nutrients. Plants without soil nutrients continue to make food in their leaves by photosynthesis, but photosynthesis alone is not enough to sustain the plants. The nutrients taken in by the roots are necessary for proper growth and maintenance of plant cells. Lack of nutrients results in many problems, including yellow leaves, wilting, thin foliage, small leaves, and generally poor growth.

Try New Approaches

Do all soils contain the same nutrients? Repeat the experiment using samples of soils taken from different locations. Remove any ground covering,

Figure 3.2

grass, and/or plants growing in the soil. Be sure to label the soil samples
and make notes of the types of plants growing in the soil and in the general area from which each sample is taken (see Figure 3.2). This information can be used later to determine the nutrients needed by these plants.
Use leached water from the different soil samples to grow plants. Determine which nutrient filtrate is the best for the plants used.

Design Your Own Experiment

Purchase an inexpensive soil nutrient-testing kit from a plant nursery or ask your teacher for a list of scientific supply houses where the kits may be obtained. Test filtrates from different soil samples for the presence of nutrients such as nitrates and phosphates. Use a data table similar to the one shown here to record the nutrients present in each soil sample and to give information about the location from which the soil is taken.

Nutrient Filtrate Data Table				
	Soil			
Nutrient	Sample 1	Sample 2	Sample 3	Sample 4
Nitrates	yes	yes	no	no
Phosphates	yes	no	no	yes

Sample 1—potting soil

Sample 2—open field with only crabgrass growing in it

Sample 3 . . .

Sample 4 . . .

Get the Facts

Use a gardening book to determine the nutrients needed for proper plant growth and the symptoms shown by a plant when there is a deficiency of each nutrient.

4 Environmental Factors and Seed Germination

Every seed that falls to the ground or that is planted does not germinate. More plants seem to grow in areas where there is an abundance of water. Is water necessary for seed germination?

In this project, you will test the effects of varying amounts of water on seed germination. You will also determine how factors such as the size of the seed, temperature, light, the depth the seed is planted, and soil affect seed germination.

Getting Started

Purpose: To determine how water affects seed germination.

Materials

3 5-ounce (150-ml) paper cups	masking tape
potting soil	distilled water
radish seeds	pencil
marking pen	saucer

Procedure

1. Fill each paper cup half full with potting soil.
2. Sprinkle the radish seeds over the surface of the soil in each cup.
3. Cover the seeds with about 1 inch (2.5 cm) of soil.
4. With the marking pen, write "Dry," "Wet," and "Moist" on pieces of masking tape and tape each label to a cup.
5. Fill the cup labeled "Wet" with distilled water. The water level should be above the surface of the soil.
6. Use the pencil to punch several holes near the bottom of the cup labeled "Moist."
7. Add distilled water to the moist cup until it begins to flow out the bottom. Set the cup in a saucer to collect any additional draining water.

Figure 4.1

8. Place all three cups in a warm area where they can remain undisturbed for seven to ten days. (See Figure 4.1.)

9. Make daily observations of the surface of the soil in each cup.

10. Record any evidence of plant growth within each cup.

Results

The rate of germination may vary, but only the seeds in the moist cup produce plants.

Why?

Seeds germinate when provided with proper amounts of moisture and oxygen at a proper temperature. In this experiment, the loose soil contains an adequate amount of oxygen, and the warm air in the room provides the proper temperature for seed germination; the factor that is missing or improper is water. The dry cup has no moisture, and the wet cup provides too much.

Without water, seeds are unable to digest the food in their tissues. Without this digested food, the seeds are unable to germinate. On the other hand, seeds require moisture but not so much that the soil becomes waterlogged, causing the excess water to displace the oxygen in the soil. Seeds cannot germinate without oxygen, and in the wet soil **anaerobic** (without oxygen) bacteria attack the seeds, causing them to die or, if they do germinate later, to develop abnormally.

Try New Approaches

1. Does the size of the seed affect the amount of water needed for germination? Repeat the experiment using larger seeds such as pinto beans or squash seeds.

2. What effect does temperature have on germination? Follow the procedure in the original experiment to prepare two containers like the moist cup. Place one cup in a refrigerator and leave one cup at room temperature. Keep the soil moist, but not dripping wet, in each cup. Check the temperature of the room and refrigerator. Observe and record your observations daily.

3. Is soil necessary for germination? Prepare several moist cups as in the original experiment filling the cups half full with materials such as gravel, stones, sand, vermiculite, paper towels, and cotton.

Design Your Own Experiment

1. Is light a factor in the germination of seeds? Fold a paper towel in half twice, moisten it with water, and sprinkle radish seeds in the center. Repeat this twice more to prepare a total of three separate paper towels with seeds. Cover one paper towel with a transparent glass plate. Cover the second paper towel with translucent wax paper. Cover the third paper towel with an opaque wrap, such as aluminum foil (see Figure 4.2). Make daily observations for seven to ten days. Display diagrams and/or photographs to document your daily observations of all three groups of seeds.

2. How does depth of planting affect germination? Plant radish seeds in sand at depths of 2 feet (60 cm), 1 foot (30 cm), 6 inches (15 cm), 4 inches (10 cm), 2 inches (5 cm), and 1 inch (2.5 cm). Tall buckets can be used to hold enough sand for the deeper plantings; paper cups, for the shallow plantings. Keep the sand damp, but not wet. Make daily observations of the surface of each container for three weeks. You want to give the seeds ample time to grow to the surface.

3. Germinating seeds live on stored energy in the cotyledons (seed leaves). Does the size of the cotyledon affect the depth that a seed can be planted? Is it possible that seeds planted too deeply germinate but that, because of their depth, the food in the cotyledons is used up before the stems reach the surface of the soil? Fold a paper towel and line the inside of a drinking glass with it. Place different-size seeds,

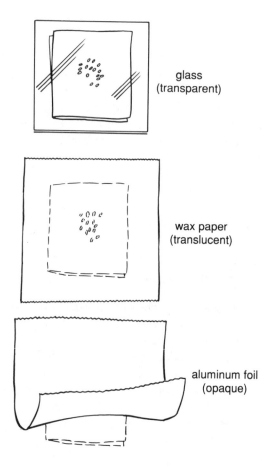

glass
(transparent)

wax paper
(translucent)

aluminum foil
(opaque)

Figure 4.2

such as pinto beans, mustard, radish, and squash seeds, at the bottom of the glass between the glass and the paper towel lining, evenly spacing the seeds around the perimeter of the glass. Wet the paper towel and keep it moist during the experiment. Cover the outside and top of the glass with black paper. The paper covering around the glass should be at least 24 inches (60 cm) high, and the cover should overlap the top to prevent light from entering (see Figure 4.3). Lift the paper cover daily to make observations. If necessary, extend the height of the paper covering. Display photographs along with a graph showing the height of each seedling to represent the results of this experiment.

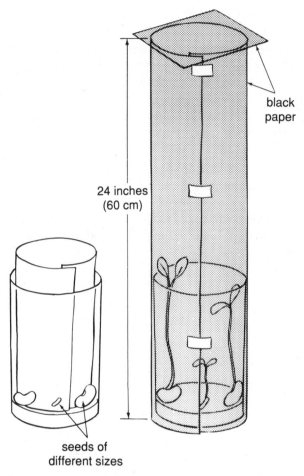

black
paper

24 inches
(60 cm)

seeds of
different sizes

Figure 4.3

Get the Facts

1. During periods of unfavorable environmental conditions, some seeds
remain dormant. In this period of rest, the seeds are said to be *queis-
cent* (at rest or motionless). They remain so until favorable conditions
arise. The length of time that seeds remain *viable* (alive and capable
of germination) varies with different species of plants. Find out more
about the viability of plants. What is the average period of viability for
seeds? How do storage conditions influence the length of the viable

period of seeds? How does the viability of South American rubber tree
seeds compare to that of Egyptian lotus seeds?

2. The environment plays an extremely important role in seed dispersal.
Some seeds are made of *hygroscopic* (readily absorbing moisture) materials that expand and contract as a result of water content. This hygroscopic mechanism allows seeds to be released during opportune
moisture conditions. Find out more about seed dispersal and the effect
of environmental conditions. How do wind and water help spread
seeds?

3. Seeds vary in the amount of heat needed for germination. Many tropi-
cal plants cannot germinate if the soil temperature falls below 50°F
(10°C). Find out more about the favorable temperatures for germination. What is the average favorable temperature range for germination
of most seeds? What are the highest and the lowest known germinating temperatures?

5 | Hydroponics: Growth without Soil

Plants need nutrients for survival. Terrestrial plants, which grow in the ground or soil, have roots to gather dissolved nutrients from the soil. But do the nutrients have to come from the soil?

In this project, you will observe hydroponic growth—that is, the growth of plants in a nutrient solution without soil. The effects of sunlight, the amount of oxygen, and the growing medium will be studied. You will also compare plants grown in soil to those grown in liquid nutrients.

Getting Started

Purpose: To construct a **hydroponicum** (hydroponic growing unit) for tomato plants.

Materials

5-gallon (20-liter) bucket

water

1-gallon (4-liter) plastic milk jug with cap

1 tablespoon (15 ml) of plant fertilizer (5–10–5)

1 teaspoon (5 ml) of Epsom salt

1 teaspoon (5 ml) of household ammonia

marking pen

masking tape

3 dwarf tomato bedding plants

scissors

3 7-oz (210-ml) paper cups

roll of paper towels

3 1-pint (500-ml) glass jars

3 1-×-1-foot (30-×-30-cm) sheets of aluminum foil

Procedure

1. Fill the bucket with tap water. Allow the water to stand in this open container for one day so that the chlorine in the water can evaporate.

2. Prepare the nutrient solution as follows:

   a. Fill the milk jug one-fourth full with dechlorinated water from the bucket.

33

   b. Add the plant fertilizer, Epsom salt, and household ammonia to
   the water in the jug. **CAUTION:** Ammonia is a poison. It and its
   fumes can damage skin and mucous membranes of nose, mouth,
   and eyes.

   c. Secure the cap and vigorously shake the jug to dissolve the
   solids.

   d. Add more water from the bucket to fill the jug to within 2 inches
   (5 cm) from the top. Rotate the jug back and forth to mix.

3. With the marking pen, write "Nutrient Solution" on a piece of masking tape and tape this label to the jug.

4. Remove one tomato plant from its bedding pot.

5. Set the plant in the bucket of dechlorinated water and gently move
it back and forth to remove as much of the soil from the roots as
possible.

6. Use scissors to cut a hole in the bottom of one paper cup just large
enough so that the tomato plant's roots fit through. You want the
roots to fit snugly in the hole with about one-fourth of the roots'
length remaining inside the cup.

7. Stuff pieces of paper towels inside the cup to give the plant support.

8. Set the paper cup inside the neck of the jar to determine how far
the bottom of the cup sits in the jar.

9. Remove the paper cup and add enough nutrient solution so that its
surface will be just beneath the bottom of the paper cup. Keep the
level of the liquid the same throughout the experiment.

10. Reposition the paper cup inside the jar (see Figure 5.1)

11. Surround the jar with one sheet of aluminum foil to prevent algae
from growing in the liquid.

12. Repeat this procedure (steps 4 through 11) for the remaining
plants.

13. Place the hydroponicums near a window in direct sunlight.

14. Keep a daily record of the growth of the plants for as long as it
takes for the plants to mature and bear fruit.

15. Place the plants in larger containers as their growth requires.

Results

Results will vary, but healthy potted plants can mature and bear fruit in a
hydroponic environment.

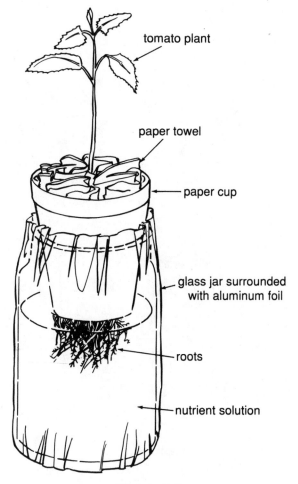

tomato plant

paper towel

paper cup

glass jar surrounded
with aluminum foil

roots

nutrient solution

Figure 5.1

Why?

Growing plants in a 100% liquid nutrient solution without a supporting medium is called **aquaponics.** In this experiment, the paper products provide support for each plant's root and stem system, but they do not add nutrients to the plant. As long as the medium in which the plant is grown does not add nutrients and all the nutrients are derived from a nutrient solution, the method of growing is considered to be hydroponic. The hydroponic growing unit, a hydroponicum, fits this description.

Figure 5.2

Try New Approaches

1. Does the amount of sunlight received by a tomato plant affect its growth? Repeat the procedure to prepare six hydroponicums of tomato bedding plants. Place two plants in each of the following situations: all day sun, morning sun, and evening sun. You may have to use shields made of boards to block the sun from directly hitting the plants that are to receive only partial sunlight (see Figure 5.2). Keep daily records. Measure the height of each plant, count the leaves, and note the general appearance of the plant's leaves and stem. **Science Fair**

Hint: Prepare and display a graph to represent the growth of each plant (see the sample graph in Figure 5.3).

2. Does the amount of oxygen received by the roots affect the growth of the plant? Prepare three hydroponicums using tomato bedding plants. Place a small aquarium aerator in each jar. Allow the liquid in the three units to be aerated for different time periods, such as 2, 8, and 24 hours.

3. Can other plants be grown hydroponically? Repeat the original experiment using bedding plants such as strawberries or flowering plants.

4. Does a growing medium affect the results? A plant can be considered hydroponically grown as long as the medium does not provide nutrients to the growing plant. Plant a tomato bedding plant in a nonnutrient medium such as LECA (light expanded clay aggregate), sand, gravel, charcoal, sawdust, and vermiculite or perlite. You could choose to use several mediums and compare their results. Use the prepared liquid nutrient from the original experiment.

Design Your Own Experiment

If the same nutrient additive is used, do terrestrial plants grow better than hydroponic plants? Plant three tomato bedding plants in soil. Follow the instructions from a professional at a nursery for the planting and care of the plants. Use the same nutrient solution to water both the plants in the hydroponicums and those in the soil. Take photographs of the different stages of growth of each plant, noting the date and time you take each photograph. Be sure to include pictures of the fruit grown from the plants. Use the sample plant growth graph (Figure 5.3) to prepare graphs for each plant. Display the photographs to represent procedure, steps and results. Display several of the graphs to show the comparison between **geoponic** (grown in the earth) and hydroponic growth.

Get the Facts

1. What nutrients are needed for proper plant growth? Use a gardening book to find the elements required for plant growth and their source and functions. What are the symptoms of specific nutrient deficiencies?

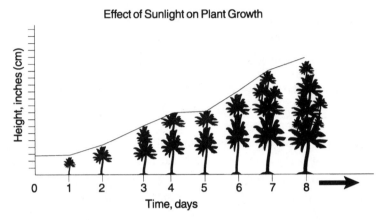

Effect of Sunlight on Plant Growth

Height, inches (cm)

Time, days

Figure 5.3

2. Seaweed is an example of growth by natural aquaponics. What other plants grow aquaponically in nature? You could display pictures of these plants to show productive aquaponic growth.

3. What are the advantages of hydroponics over geoponics? Find out more about growing plants in liquid instead of soil. Is it more or less expensive? Is it more productive? Is it more environmentally sound?

6 | Cell Homeostasis: A Steady State

The survival of living cells greatly depends on their capacity to achieve homeostasis. The ability of a cell to regulate a stable internal environment is accomplished by controlling the movement of materials through the cell membrane. When this delicate balance is lost, the cell can be injured and even die.

In this project, you will study osmosis and determine how placing cells into hypotonic and hypertonic solutions affects osmosis. The rate of water movement through the cell membrane of an egg will be calculated, and factors affecting osmotic and turgor pressure will be studied.

Getting Started

Purpose: To determine the effect of placing a cell into a **hypotonic solution** (a solution with a high concentration of water as compared to that in the cell).

Materials

baby food jar with small mouth

distilled water

raw egg in shell

metal spoon

drinking straw (clear or transparent)

8-inch (20-cm) candle (or longer)

matches

CAUTION: Always wash your hands after touching an uncooked egg. It may contain harmful bacteria.

Procedure

1. Fill the baby food jar three-fourths full with distilled water.
2. Gently tap the rounded end of the egg's shell with the edge of the spoon.
3. Use your fingernails to carefully pull away several small pieces of the eggshell. *Note:* You want to remove a small section of the shell about the size of the tip of your finger. Be careful not to pierce the thin membrane under the shell.
4. On the opposite end of the egg, break a hole in the shell large enough to insert the end of the straw.

  5. Stand the egg in the jar of water, rounded end down.
  6. Insert about 1 inch (2.5 cm) of one end of the straw into the hole in the shell and through the cell membrane.
  7. Light the candle and hold the unlit end.
  8. Allow the melted wax to drip around the base of the straw until the space between the straw and the eggshell is sealed (see Figure 6.1).
  9. Allow the egg and attached straw to stand undisturbed overnight.
  10. Observe any movement of liquid.

Results

A clear, watery liquid moves up the drinking straw.

Why?

Cell **homeostasis** is the ability of a cell to achieve a stable internal environment by regulating the passage of fluids through the cell membrane. Removing the eggshell exposes the semipermeable membrane of the cell (a hen's egg is a single cell). A **semipermeable membrane** is a membrane through which some substances can pass but others cannot. Water molecules are small enough to move through the membrane, but larger molecules inside the cell are too large to move out of the cell. The movement of water through the membrane is called **osmosis.**

Osmosis occurs when there is a difference in the concentration of water on either side of the membrane. The water concentration in the jar is 100%. The water concentration inside the egg is less than 100% because of the dissolved fats, proteins, and other materials. Water moves through any cell membrane from an area of high water concentration to an area of low water concentration. Thus, the water in the jar moves through the exposed membrane of the egg and into the egg. As water enters the egg, the volume of fluid increases and the extra molecules are forced up the straw. This force is produced by **osmotic pressure** (the pressure of water diffusing through the semipermeable membrane). The greater the difference in water concentration on either side of the membrane, the greater the osmotic pressure.

Try New Approaches

  1. How long does it take to fill the egg to capacity? Repeat the experiment measuring the time from the moment the egg is placed into the water until liquid is seen at the base of the straw.

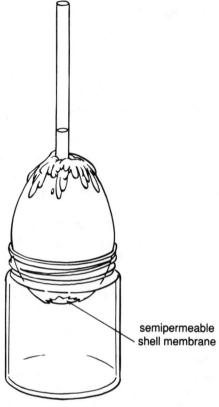

Figure 6.1

2. Does the surface area of the membrane affect the rate the water flows into the egg? Repeat the original experiment exposing more of the membrane by breaking away larger pieces of the shell. Again, measure the time needed for the egg to fill to capacity. **Science Fair Hint:** Prepare an egg with a straw for display. Show photographs to represent the various experiments and their results.

3. Once the egg is filled to capacity, at what rate does the water flow into the egg? Does the rate continue to remain the same? To find the answers to these questions, use an egg that is filled to capacity. Use a marking pen to mark the liquid level in the straw every hour for eight hours or until the straw is filled. Use the distances between the hourly markings to determine whether the flow rate is constant. **Science Fair Hint:** Include diagrams showing the height of the liquid in the straw in the project report as well as part of the project display.

Design Your Own Experiment

1. Do cells **dehydrate** (lose water) when placed into **hypertonic solutions** (solutions with low concentrations of water)? Mix 1 tablespoon (15 ml) of table salt (sodium chloride) with 1 cup (250 ml) of water. Pour the salt solution into a bowl. Cut four slices from a potato, each about ¼ inch (6 mm) thick. Place the potato slices into the salty water. After 15 minutes, cut another slice from the potato and test the firmness of this potato slice by trying to bend the slice back and forth with your fingers. Test the firmness of the potato slices in the salt solution. A lack of firmness indicates that water has moved out of the cells. Thus, the cells have lost **turgor pressure** (pressure inside cells due to the presence of water). Try testing different objects and solutions. Display diagrams to represent your results.

2. What happens to plants that live in fresh water? What stops the water from flowing into their cells? Prepare a wet-mount slide of one leaf of elodea. See Appendix 1 for instructions on preparing slides. Use a microscope to examine the slide. With low- and high-power magnification, observe the structure of each cell and notice the cell wall. Remove the water from the cells by adding drops of a table salt solution [made with 1 tablespoon (15 ml) of sodium chloride in ½ cup (125 ml) of water at the edge of the coverslip] (see Figure 6.2). Observe the structure of the cell in the salt solution. Remove the salt solution by placing a paper towel at the edge of the coverslip. Add drops of distilled water at the edge of the coverslip while watching the cell through the microscope. You should observe that the cells shrink in the salt solution and expand in the water. They rarely expand enough to rupture, however, because of the strong pressure of the outer cellulose walls. When the pressure within the cell equals the osmotic pressure, the water no longer enters or leaves the cell.

Get the Facts

1. Fresh-water animals, such as fish and protozoans, do not have strong cellulose walls to protect them from water that continually enters due to osmotic pressure. How do the cells of these organisms protect themselves? Find out how energy is employed to pump the excess water back out into the environment. What is a *contractile vacuole,* what organisms have it, and how does it function?

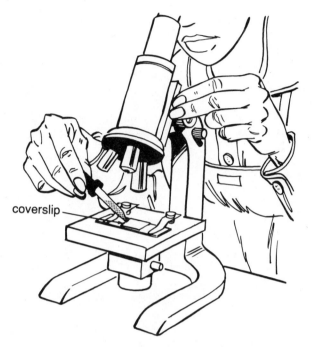

coverslip

Figure 6.2

2. Why does a fresh-water plant wilt when placed in salty water, while marine organisms survive daily in salty sea water? What does it mean when we say that sea water is *isotonic* to the cytoplasm of sea organisms but *hypertonic* to the cytoplasm of fresh-water organisms? What is *plasmolysis*?

3. The human kidney continuously filters blood, removes wastes, and maintains a proper salt-and-water balance. An artificial kidney machine is used to perform these same functions. How does this machine work? How does the machine use the process of osmosis to cleanse the blood?

7 | Effect of Water on Turgor Pressure

The stiffness of plant stems, roots, and leaves is due to the presence of water in their cells. Plants exhibit turgor when they stand erect and return to their original position after being bent. This rigidity in plants is the result of the firmness of each water-filled cell.

In this project, you will determine the changes in turgor pressure in plants as a result of increases and decreases of water concentration in a plant's cells. Factors affecting the absorption of water into cells, such as variations in cell types, temperature, and permeability of the cell membrane, will be determined. You will also study the effect of turgor pressure on plant movement.

Getting Started

Purpose: To demonstrate the effects of turgor pressure on an animal cell membrane.

Materials

baby food jar	refrigerator
white vinegar	1-cup (250-ml) measuring cup
raw egg in shell	distilled water

CAUTION: Always wash your hands after touching an uncooked egg. It may contain harmful bacteria.

Procedure

1. Fill the jar with vinegar.

2. Stand the egg in the jar of vinegar with the small end of the egg below the surface of the vinegar (see Figure 7.1).

3. Put the jar and the egg in the refrigerator to prevent the egg from spoiling.

4. After 24 hours, remove the egg and discard the vinegar.

5. Carefully place the egg into the measuring cup without cracking the eggshell.

6. Fill the cup with distilled water.

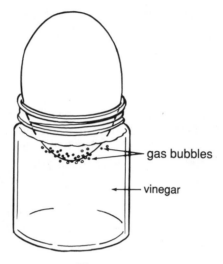

gas bubbles

vinegar

Figure 7.1

7. Put the cup in the refrigerator.

8. Observe the egg for seven days.

Results

The membrane exposed by the vinegar swells and finally ruptures. Cracks in the shell starting at the edge of the exposed membrane form and extend across the egg. (See Figure 7.2.)

Why?

The egg is a single cell surrounded by a cell membrane. This membrane—the shell membrane—surrounds and controls the passage of materials into and out of the egg.

Membranes that are selective in what passes through them are called semipermeable membranes. Pores in the membranes are large enough to allow the easy passage of water molecules, but they are too small to allow larger molecules such as fats and proteins to get through. The movement of water through a cell membrane is called osmosis and occurs when there is a difference in the concentration of water on either side of the membrane.

The swollen shell membrane ruptures when placed into a hypotonic solution (a solution with a higher water concentration than that of the area to which it is compared). The water in the cup (100% water) is hypo-

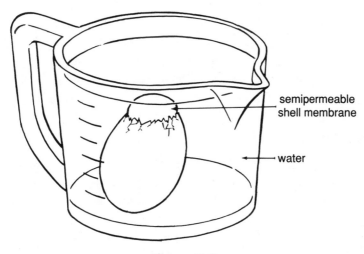

Figure 7.2

tonic to the fluid content of the egg. As more water moves into the egg through the membrane, the cell becomes crowded with excess molecules, which results in a buildup of pressure. This pressure caused by excess water is called turgor pressure. As the fluid content of the egg continues to increase, the pressure of the expanding shell membrane breaks the hard eggshell. The thin, unprotective shell membrane stretches under the pressure, creating a bulge that ultimately ruptures.

Try New Approaches

1. How do the results change when the egg is placed into a hypertonic solution (a solution with a lower water concentration than that of the area to which it is compared)? Repeat the experiment replacing the distilled water with a salt solution made with 1 cup (250 ml) of water and 1 tablespoon (15 ml) of table salt (sodium chloride). **Science Fair Hint:** Use a data table to record written descriptions and diagrams of observations made of eggs placed into hypertonic and hypotonic solutions.

2. If more of the membrane is exposed, does the egg continue to swell and rupture when placed into a hypotonic solution? Repeat the original experiment removing the entire shell from the egg by covering the egg with white vinegar for 24 hours. Measure the circumference of the egg before placing it into the vinegar (mixture of acetic acid and water) and before placing it into the water. After placing it in the water, measure it daily for seven days or until the egg breaks (if it does). Use these measurements to determine the change in size of the cell due to osmosis and whether the water continues to enter the cell at an even rate each day.

Design Your Own Experiment

1. What is the effect of turgor pressure on plant cells? Demonstrate the change in turgor pressure in plant cells by cutting across the bottom of different plant stems, such as flowers and celery. Stand the stalks in an empty glass at room temperature. Prepare a second stalk of each plant in like manner, but stand these stalks in a glass half filled with distilled water. Allow the stems to stand in the glasses for 24 hours. Observe the change in the appearance and firmness of the stalks. Display before and after photographs of the stalks to represent the changes of turgor pressure as a result of the gain and loss of water from cells.

2. How does turgor pressure affect the movement of plants? Water movement through the petals of morning glories creates enough pressure to cause the petals to spread open. Cut a 6-×-2-inch (15-×-5-cm) strip from a newspaper. Cut a petal shape at both ends of the strip. Fold the petals toward the center of the strip and crease the paper so that the petals lay flat. Drop the folded paper, petal side up, on top of water in a bowl (see Figure 7.3). Notice what happens. More information about the opening of flowers due to turgor pressure can be found in the experiment titled "Morning Glory," (p. 30) in Janice VanCleave's *200 Gooey, Slippery, Slimy, Weird, and Fun Experiments* (New York: Wiley, 1992).

3. How does heat affect the rate and quantity of water absorption by cells? Into each of three Styrofoam® cups, pour cold, room-temperature, and warm water, respectively. Place raisins and a thermometer in each cup. *Note:* Do not make the water so hot that it ruptures the cell membrane of the fruit. Use aluminum foil to seal off the top of the cups. Observe the size of the raisins in each cup as often as possible until the temperature of the water in the cups is the same. Use your observations to determine whether the temperature affected the rate and quantity of water absorbed by the raisins.

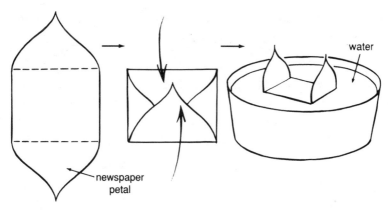

water

newspaper
petal

Figure 7.3

4. Membranes of cells continue to be semipermeable as long as they are alive, but liquids are easily extracted from plants after their tissues have been killed. Demonstrate this by using two fresh beets. Grate one of the beets and boil the second beet in a saucepan of water. Even when grated, the fresh beet cells retain their fluids, but much of the liquid coloring matter inside the beet is extracted by killing the cells in the hot water.

Get the Facts

1. Osmotic pressure can move small quantities of water into stems, but the tons of water raised to the tops of giant sequoias and even the small quantities of water lifted to the petals of morning glories require more than osmotic pressure. Plants do not pull or pump the water through their systems, but the water does flow up the stems of plants. The movement of this water to the summit of giant trees or the top of small plants is a result of transpiration, capillary action, cohesion, and adhesion. Find out more about this upward movement of water against the downward pull of gravity.

2. Effective responses in animals require internal communication. The nervous systems in higher organisms send messages that result in movement due to muscle relaxation and contraction. Plants have no nervous systems or muscle cells, and quick responses are almost nonexistent in the plant kingdom. However, a few plants, such as the mimosa, respond rapidly to being touched. It appears that a stimulus passes through the plant's stem as the leaves fold in a wave of motion from the tip to the base. Find out more about rapid plant motion. What causes this rapid movement of mimosa leaves? Nerves are not involved, but are there any electrical impulses in plants? Is this motion due to tropism or nastic movements?

8 Asexual Reproduction

There are two basic types of reproduction of living organisms. One type, sexual reproduction, requires the union of male and female sex cells, or gametes (sperm and eggs) in the formation of a new organism.

In this project, you will study the second type of reproduction, asexual reproduction, where there is no union of sex cells. The ability of plants to reproduce asexually by vegetative propagation will be studied. You will also discover some methods and special plant organs by which plants can asexually reproduce.

Getting Started

Purpose: To produce a new plant by fragmentation.

Materials

2 1-quart (1-liter) jars
distilled water

scissors
geranium plant

Procedure

1. Fill the jars three-fourths full with distilled water.
2. Use the scissors to cut four healthy stems with healthy leaves from the geranium plant.
3. Place two stems, cut ends down, into each jar of distilled water (see A in Figure 8.1).
4. Place the jars where they will receive direct sunlight.
5. Observe the cut ends of the stems daily for two to three weeks.
6. Transfer the cuttings to flowerpots filled with potting soil for further growth.
7. Keep the plants watered and observe their growth for several months.

Results

In 10 to 14 days, small roots can be seen growing from the ends of the stems (see B in Figure 8.1). These roots continue to grow. The potted stems mature into plants resembling the original (parent) plant.

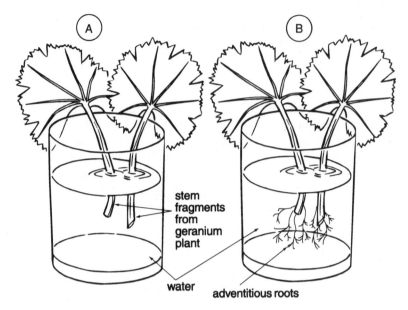

Figure 8.1

Why?

Asexual reproduction is a method of reproducing a new organism from one parent. One type of asexual reproduction is **vegetative propagation** (the production of a new organism from a nonsexual part of one parent). In multicelled organisms such as plants, broken pieces from the plants can develop into new plants. Special roots called **adventitious roots** develop directly from stems or leaves instead of from the normal root system.

Fragmentation is an example of vegetative asexual reproduction. In this process, a new plant grows from a part broken from a parent plant. The cutting taken from the geranium plant grows into a plant identical to the parent plant.

Asexual reproduction has several advantages. First, this method can be used to grow identical plants faster and more successfully than a method that relies on seed germination. Second, seedless fruit can be produced and propagated via vegetative reproduction. Third, asexual reproduction preserves the status quo in that the offspring are always exactly like the parent.

Try New Approaches

1. Do leaves affect the ability of a stem to reproduce by fragmentation? Repeat the experiment two times, first using stems with no leaves, and then using stems with a greater number of leaves than the stems used in the original experiment.

2. Does the type of plant affect its ability to reproduce by fragmentation? Repeat the original experiment using stems from different types of houseplants. Discuss the project with a professional at a nursery and secure sample cuttings from different types of plants.

3. For vegetative propagation to occur, adventitious roots must form. The development of these special roots depends on a hormone called **auxin.** Can the hastening of the production of adventitious roots be achieved by pretreating the cuttings with a synthetic auxin solution? Repeat the original experiment using synthetic auxin purchased from a nursery. Follow the procedure on the product's packaging for treating the cuttings.

Design Your Own Experiment

What parts of a plant can grow into an offspring? The following procedures allow you to determine the ability of plants to propagate from roots, stems, and leaves.

1. Grow plants from carrot tops (roots) by filling a shallow container with sand (see Figure 8.2). Thoroughly wet the sand with water and insert the cut end of the carrot tops into the wet sand. Place the container in a lighted area and keep the sand wet. Observe the tops of the carrots for several weeks. Transfer them to a deeper container for further maturing of the plants. Check with a professional at a nursery for the best growing soil for carrots.

2. Bulbs are plants with short, underground stems and thick fleshy leaves. The leaves store food for the growth of the plant. Plant several bulbs, such as onions, tulips, daffodils, or lilies, in potting soil. After two weeks, make daily observations of one of the bulbs by removing and carefully brushing away the soil. Allow the other bulbs to continue growing undisturbed.

3. Tubers, such as white potatoes, are plants with swollen, underground stems. The "eyes" on a potato are tuber buds from which a new plant

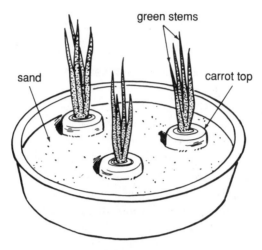

Figure 8.2

will grow. Leave some potatoes in a closed cabinet for several weeks. Make daily observations of the eyes on the potatoes. Other ways to propagate plants from potatoes include the following:

a. Cut the eyes from the potato and plant them in soil.

b. Place four toothpicks around the center of a sweet potato and place the potato, pointed side down, into a jar of water (see Figure 8.3).

4. Place a bryophyllum or jade plant leaf on the surface of potting soil. Keep the soil moist and observe the edges of the leaf.

Display photographs of the different stages of development of the plants in each of the preceding experiments. Display the pictures along with data tables of daily growth measurements. Use the healthier plants as part of the project display.

Get the Facts

1. All McIntosh apple trees are clones of an original tree found 150 years ago on the farm of John McIntosh in Ontario, Canada. This cloning has been accomplished by *grafting*. Find out more about the grafting of plants. What is a *scion*? Why is the stock often grown from seed? What are the advantages of grafting?

2. Strawberries grow from runners. *Runners* are stems that grow horizontally rather than vertically. Find out more about this type of vegeta-

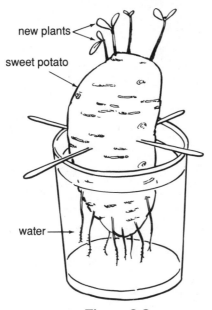

Figure 8.3

tive propagation. What are *rhizomes*? How does a *stolon* differ from
a rhizome?

3. Spores are small bodies containing a nucleus and a small amount of
cytoplasm. Find out more about *sporulation,* the asexual production of
spores. How do spores ensure survival of the plant during unfavorable
environmental conditions? What type of plant produces spores?

4. German biologist Theodor Boveri's experiments showed that heredi-
tary is a result of the nuclear material called *chromosomes.* Through
the continuous process of cell division called *mitosis,* the blueprint material in chromosomes is duplicated. Use a biology text to find out
more about Boveri's experiment and about the process of mitosis. How
many steps are in the process? What happens in each step?

9 | Apical Dominance: Growth Inhibitor

Certain plant hormones known as auxins are responsible for many plant responses. Auxins affect, for example, the growth of buds, stems, leaves, and roots.

In this project, you will have the opportunity to demonstrate apical dominance, which is the inhibition of lateral bud development by the growth of a terminal shoot—an effect caused by auxins. You will also study the effects of auxins on plant activities such as the stimulation of fruit development and the shedding of leaves and fruit (abscission).

Getting Started

Purpose: To determine whether the terminal bud on a white potato exhibits apical dominance.

Materials

marking pen   baking pan

10 white potatoes

Procedure

1. Use the marking pen to number each potato.

2. Observe and record the appearance of each potato.

3. Place the potatoes side by side on the baking pan. Try to give them as much space as possible.

4. Set the pan in a closed cabinet.

5. Observe and record the appearance of the potatoes weekly until a 6-inch (15-cm) growth of one of the buds is observed. This could take three or more weeks.

6. When observing the bud growth, be very careful not to break any buds. *Note:* Save the potatoes for later experiments.

Results

A bud on the end of the potato grows into a long shoot, but the other bud growth is shorter.

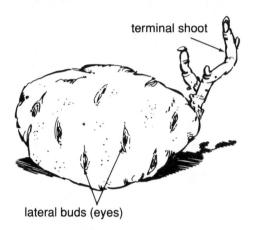

terminal shoot

lateral buds (eyes)

Figure 9.1

Why?

A potato is actually part of the underground stem of a potato plant. The buds on a potato are often called "eyes." The eye at the end of the potato that develops into a long shoot is a **terminal** (apical) bud; the remaining eyes are referred to as **lateral** buds because they grow from the side of the stem (see Figure 9.1).

The growth of the terminal bud on the potato and on other plant stems generally inhibits the development of the lateral buds on the stem below. This inhibition of lateral shoot growth because of the presence of a terminal shoot is called **apical dominance.** Apical dominance is more pronounced in plants that have tall, single stems (such as pine trees), but even short, bushy shrubs can develop a single terminal shoot. Gardeners prune the terminal shoots from shrubs and trees to make the plants' lower stems grow. They know that fuller trees and bushes result if the terminal shoots are cut.

Removal of the terminal shoot affects the distribution of auxin (a hormone that causes the cells in a plant to lengthen) in the stem. Apical dominance is thought to be the result of the production of auxin in the meristem cells of the terminal bud that are then transported downward. **Meristem** cells are located at the top of each stem, and it is these cells that divide by a process called **mitosis.** The cell division in the meristem of apical buds is stimulated by the presence of auxin, but the downward transport of auxin produced in the apical buds inhibits cell division in the lateral buds.

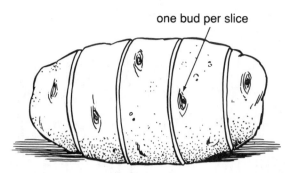

Figure 9.2

Try New Approaches

1. Can lateral buds develop without the presence of a terminal shoot? Repeat the experiment two times, first using slices from potatoes with developing shoots, and then using slices from potatoes with undeveloped buds. For the first experiment, use several potatoes from the original experiment that have well-developed terminal shoots and partially developing lateral shoots. Cut ten sections from the potatoes, one shoot to a section. Break off any extra shoots so that there is only one shoot per slice. For the second experiment, use several potatoes not from the original experiment that do not have developing shoots. Cut ten sections from the potatoes, one bud to a section (see Figure 9.2).

2a. Do lateral buds develop if the terminal bud is removed? Repeat the original experiment. As the buds develop, remove the dominant terminal buds from all but two of the potatoes. These two will be the controls. **Science Fair Hint:** As the buds develop, measure the shoots on the potatoes and use graphs to represent the growth of shoots with and without the terminal shoots.

b. When the terminal shoot is removed, do any of the lateral shoots become more prolific and reimpose apical dominance? As the preceding experiment progresses, observe the lengths of the shoots and determine whether one or more shoots on the potatoes begin to outgrow the others and replace the removed terminal shoots (see Figure 9.3).

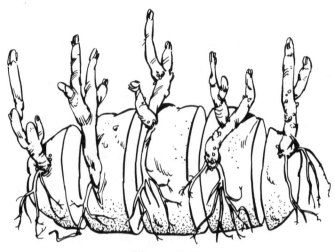

Figure 9.3

Design Your Own Experiment

Does the auxin in commercial products such as blossom set actually prevent fruit from prematurely falling from a plant? Is it possible that the plant would produce its own auxin if provided with the proper nutrients? Grow tomato plants in soil with varying amounts of nitrogen and phosphorous. With the assistance of a professional at a nursery, select at least eight dwarf tomato plants that can be grown in large buckets and choose nitrogen- and phosphorus-rich fertilizers and a prepared product designed to set the blossoms on tomato plants. Divide the plants into two groups. At the time suggested on the blossom-set product label, spray half of the plants in each group. The table on the next page indicates the different nitrogen (N) and phosphorus (P) levels that each plant receives. It is also a sample data table that you can use when recording and displaying your results.

Get the Facts

1. A chemical growth stimulator called *auxin* seems to affect fruit development, apical dominance, *abscission, positive and negative tropism,* and other plant growth. Use biology texts to find out more about the discovery and role of auxin. Describe and even duplicate the experiments of early scientists such as Charles Darwin, Peter Boysen–Jensen, and F. W. Went.

Fruit Development Data Table		
Fertilizer Content	Plants in Group 1 without blossom set	Plants in Group 2 with blossom set
high P, low N		
high P, high N		
low P, high N		
no fertilizer		

2. In the fall, leaves from deciduous trees drop off. Auxin plays an important role in *abscission*. As long as leaves and fruits produce auxin, they remain firmly attached to their stems. Auxin appears to be produced in leaves and fruits, and reduction of the hormone causes abscission. Find out what stimuli trigger the reduction of auxin production. What is the importance of leaf drop? How is it a valuable adaptation for deciduous trees? How do the shape and the texture of nondeciduous plant leaves make annual fall leaf drop unnecessary?

Transportation System in Vascular Plants

10

Plant cells must receive water, nutrients, oxygen, and food and have wastes (such as carbon dioxide) removed. In vascular plants, xylem and phloem, miniature tubelike tissues, transport materials throughout the parts of the plants.

In this project, you will demonstrate how liquids move through vascular plants that have fibrovascular bundles consisting of xylem, phloem, and supportive fibers. You will also determine factors affecting the rate of translocation, such as the presence of leaves, light, and humidity.

Getting Started

Purpose: To demonstrate the transportation of liquid through a plant's vascular system.

Materials

one clear drinking glass

water

red food coloring

knife

2 fresh stalks of celery with leaves (preferably the pale innermost stalks)

Procedure

1. Fill the glass about one-fourth full with water.
2. Add enough food coloring to make the water in the glass a deep red color.
3. Use the knife to cut across the bottom end of each celery stalk.
4. Stand the cut end of the stalks in the glass of colored water.
5. Observe and record the appearance of the stalks every hour for the first three hours. Make as many additional observations as often as possible during the first 12 hours. Be sure to record the time of each observation, starting with zero and indicating the amount of

Transportation Data Chart

Time	Observations		Diagram
	Stem	Leaves	
0	pale green	pale green	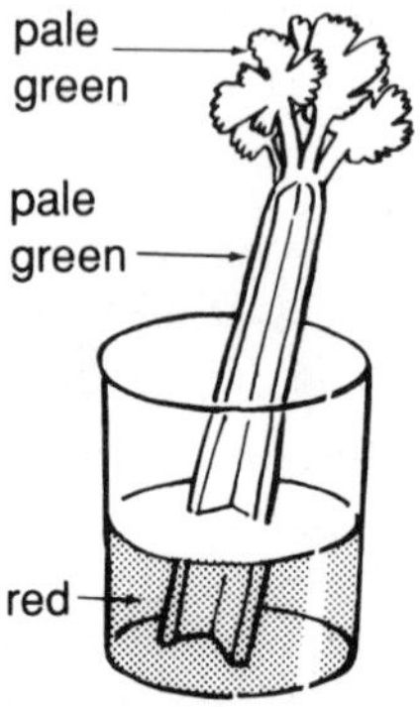 pale green / pale green / red
12 hours	green with pale red stripes running up the stalk	reddish	Note: Draw a colored diagram here.

Figure 10.1

time that passes between each of the observations described. Include diagrams as part of the descriptions (see the sample data table in Figure 10.1).

6. After 12 hours, remove one stalk of celery from the glass.

7. Observe and record the appearance of the outside of this stalk.

8. Use the knife to cut slices across the stalk. Remove sections 1 inch (2.5 cm) long from the bottom, middle, and top of the stalk. Observe and record the appearance of the slices.

9. After 24 hours, observe the outside of the stalk still standing in the colored water.

10. Cut three sections from this stalk as before (step 8). Observe and record their appearance.

Results

During the first three hours, a faint red color can be seen rising up the stalks. After 12 hours, the leaves are reddish in color, and slices taken from the stalk reveal tiny red dots spaced around the outside edges. After 24 hours, the leaves show more of a red hue, but the stalk slices appear the same.

Why?

Vascular plants are plants that have special tissues for transporting food, minerals, and water (a system called **translocation**). These vascular tissues are made up of bundles of tubes. **Phloem** tubes transport food manufactured in the leaves to other parts of the plant. The movement of water from the roots to the leaves is accomplished by **xylem** tubes. This upward movement of water against the downward pull of gravity is the result of capillary action and transpiration.

 Capillary action is the rising of a liquid in small tubes because of adhesive and cohesive forces. **Adhesion** is the attraction between dissimilar molecules such as the attraction that water molecules have for the molecules that make up the sides of the xylem tubes. **Cohesion** is the attraction between similar molecules such as the attraction that water molecules have for one another. The adhesive attraction of the water molecules to the sides of the tubes moves the water up the sides of the tubes. The water molecules clinging to the tubes then pull the water below up the center of the tubes.

 Transpiration is the evaporation of water through leaf pores called **stomata**. As the water evaporates from the plant, more water molecules are pulled in at the roots; thus, a continuous flow of water enters the roots and rises in the xylem, bringing necessary nutrients dissolved in the water to the plant. This movement is evident by the intensifying of the red color in the leaves.

Try New Approaches

Will water rise in a celery stalk without any leaves? Remove all of the leaves from two celery stalks and use them to repeat the experiment.

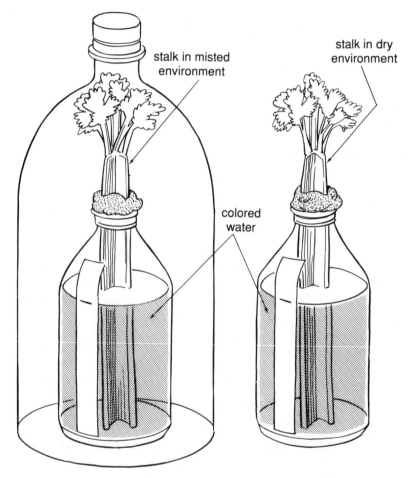

stalk in misted environment

stalk in dry environment

colored water

Figure 10.2

Use the knife to cut across both the top and bottom of each stalk. Make observations of the tops of the stalks.

Design Your Own Experiment

1. How does humidity affect the rate of transpiration? Fill two small glass soda bottles half full with red-colored water. Stand one stalk of celery with leaves in each bottle. Use modeling clay as a seal around the mouth of each bottle. With masking tape and a marking pen, mark the water level of the liquid in each bottle. Use scissors to cut off the bottom of a clear, 2-liter plastic soda bottle. Secure the cap on this bottle and place it over one of the bottles containing a celery stalk (see Figure 10.2). Raise the plastic bottle and, using a spray bottle, mist the air inside the plastic bottle twice a day, morning and evening, for one week. Place the second bottle containing a celery stalk in a dry place. At the end of the week, compare the water level of the bottle in the misted environment to that of the bottle in the dry environment.

2. Do plants transpire more at night or during the day? Select one leaf on each of two identical plants. Choose leaves that are of equal size. Place a clear plastic sandwich bag over each leaf and secure the bags to the stems with masking tape. Place both plants near a window that receives direct sunlight. Cover one of the plants with a cardboard box. After three hours, observe the inside of each bag.

Get the Facts

1. *Gluttation* is the early morning release of liquid water at the edges of plant leaves. What causes this water release?

2. Vascular plants have xylem and phloem tubes. What is the difference in the structure of these two sets of tubes? You could use diagrams to represent the difference in the cell structure of xylem and phloem tubes.

3. *Girding* a tree means stripping away a continuous ring of bark. This procedure affects the phloem ring and thus interrupts the translocation of nutrients. How does girding affect the growth of the tree? What causes the bulge in the bark above the wound made by girding?

Direction of Growth of Roots, Stems, and Leaves

11

All parts of a plant grow. Plant stems and roots elongate in predetermined directions (up and down, respectively). The stems and roots also increase in diameter, and leaves increase in surface area.

In this project, you will have the opportunity to observe the direction of root, stem, and leaf growth. You will also determine the location of any new growth of these three plant organs. The growing point of these three plant organs will be determined. You will also look at factors affecting growth, such as temperature, light, and plant types.

Getting Started

Purpose: To observe the elongation of a **dicot** (plant that has seeds with two seed leaves) plant stem and to determine whether the entire stem of the plant is vegetative.

Materials

3 7-ounce (210-ml) paper cups	12 pole pinto beans
potting soil	water
ruler	marking pen
pencil	

Procedure

1. Fill each paper cup with potting soil to within 1 inch (2.5 cm) from the top.
2. Use the pencil to punch four to six holes near the bottom of each cup.
3. Lay four beans on the surface of the soil in each cup.
4. Cover the beans with about 1 inch (2.5 cm) of soil.
5. Moisten the soil with water.

6. Allow the seeds to germinate and the seedlings to grow to a height of about 6 inches (15 cm) above the top of each cup. *Note:* This will take from five to seven days.

7. Use the marking pen to mark a line across the stem of each plant level with the lip of the cup. Use this line as the starting line.

8. Mark three equal sections on each stem between the cotyledons (part of the seed that contains stored food for the plant embryo), or seed leaves, and the starting line (see Figure 11.1).

9. Mark three equal sections on each stem between the cotyledons and the true leaves at the top of the stem.

10. Prepare drawings of each plant, numbering each section from 1 to 6, starting at the top of each stem as in Figure 11.1.

11. Measure and record the length of each section.

12. At the same time each day for seven days, measure and record the length of each section again.

Results

The author's plants showed the greatest elongation in the sections marked 1, only slight changes in the sections marked 2, and no measurable changes in the lower sections marked 3 through 6.

Why?

Elongation of plant stems occurs primarily in the meristems. Meristem is a term derived from the Greek word *meristos,* which means "divided." The **apical** part of the stem (near the tip) has the meristematic cells (cells that divide), and it is at the tip where the growth of the stem occurs.

Cell division is carried out by a process called mitosis. In mitosis, the cell parts duplicate themselves and then divide into two separate cells. This division and duplication process occurs in meristematic cells. As the stem grows, small masses of meristematic cells are left behind, and it is at these points that branches and leaves develop.

Try New Approaches

1. Does the rate of meristematic growth change during different periods of the day? Repeat the experiment using only the sections of the stems above the cotyledons. Measure these sections at two-hour intervals during the day, starting early and stopping as late as possible. Prepare a data table of the results similar to the one shown on page 72.

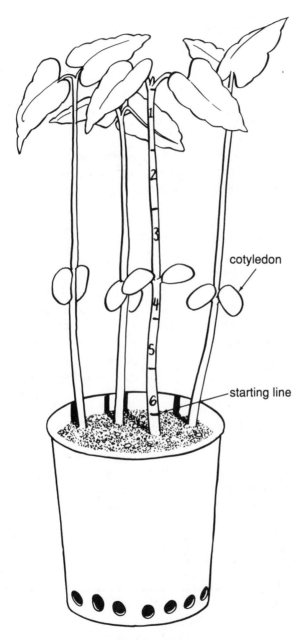

Figure 11.1

Meristem Growth Table			
Time	Section 1	Section 2	Section 3
8:00 A.M.			
10:00 A.M.			

2. Does light duration affect the rate of meristematic growth? **Photoperiodism** is the development of an organism depending on the duration of daylight or darkness. Test the effect of light or its absence by repeating the original experiment using three test groups of plants. Make every effort to vary only the amount of light that each group receives. Place one group near a window to receive sunlight, the second group under artificial lighting 24 hours a day, and the third group in a dark closet. Measure the plants daily.

3. Does the length of the stem tip actually involved in the growing process vary in different plants? Repeat the original experiment using seedlings from different plants. Divide the stem section above the cotyledon leaves into six parts to make a better comparison of the length of the growing area on the tips of each type of plant. **Science Fair Hint:** Use diagrams showing the changes in the length of each section as part of a project display.

4. Does temperature affect the growth of meristematic cells? Repeat the original experiment to prepare three plants for study. Design a method so that the growing conditions (water, light, nutrients, and so on) for each plant are the same except for temperature. You could make miniature plastic greenhouses using ice cubes to cool one greenhouse, direct sun to warm another, and a shaded area that gets indirect sun for the third.

Design Your Own Experiment

1. Is the elongation of roots a result of apical meristem division? Place a folded paper towel on a 1-×-1-foot (30-×-30-cm) sheet of aluminum foil. Moisten the paper towel with water. Position six pinto beans in a straight line across the center of the wet paper towel. Fold the foil around the towel and close up each end of the foil. Stand the foil package in a glass. After five days, open the foil package and use a marking

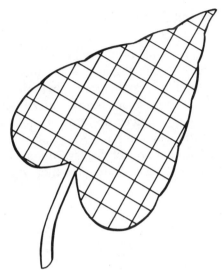

Figure 11.2

pen to divide the roots into three equal sections. Open the package each day for one week and measure and compare the lengths of each section. **Science Fair Hint:** Use photographs and drawings of the development of the roots as project displays. They would be especially useful in presenting the procedure steps and results of the experiment.

2. What part of a leaf expands? Use a ruler and a marking pen to draw a grid on several leaves of different bean seedlings (see Figure 11.2). Determine the average surface area of each leaf by multiplying the length by the average width. Calculate the average surface area of the leaves each day for one week. **Science Fair Hint:** Use a series of drawings to represent the regions of expansion on the leaves.

Get the Facts

1. Plants grow by cell enlargement and cell division. Biology texts can give you information about these two processes. First, find out how a cell, starting with a fixed amount of protoplasm within its walls, can grow by elongation. Second, discover the steps involved in the actual division of cells by the process of mitosis.

2. New cells in plants are produced in meristems. These tissues are located where new growth begins on roots and stems. Find out more

about these special cells. How do they compare with other cells in the plant?

3. In dicots, the growth in diameter of stems and roots is accomplished by a band of *cambium* (plant tissue that produces new xylem and phloem cells). Mitosis in the cambium results in the expansion of the stem or root. Find out more about the growth in diameter of stems and roots. Exactly what produces the growth rings seen in a cross-sectional slice from the trunk of a tree? If available, you could use a slice from a tree trunk in a project display. Monocots lack cambium. How do these plants increase in diameter without cambium?

Geotropism: Plant Movement Due to Gravity

12

Plants do not move from one location to another, but their leaves, stems, and roots do move. These parts of plants move at such a slow rate that the motion is not noticed. Movement in plants is a response to stimuli, and this movement, or tropism, will be either toward or away from the particular stimulus. Positive tropism is a movement toward the stimulus, and negative tropism is a movement away from the stimulus.

In this project, you will learn about geotropism, the response of plants to gravity. You will also determine which parts of a plant exhibit positive and negative geotropism as well as how plants behave in a simulated-gravity environment.

Getting Started

Purpose: To determine how gravity affects plant growth.

Materials

paper towel	mustard seeds
12-×-12-inch (30-×-30-cm) sheet of aluminum foil	marking pen
	1-quart (1-liter) jar
tap water	

Procedure

1. Fold the paper towel in half twice.
2. Place the folded paper towel in the center of the aluminum foil.
3. Moisten the paper towel with tap water so that it is damp, but not dripping wet.
4. Sprinkle mustard seeds in a line across the center of the damp paper towel (see A in Figure 12.1).
5. Fold the foil around the towel and close up each end of the foil.
6. Use the marking pen to draw an arrow on the outside of the foil package.

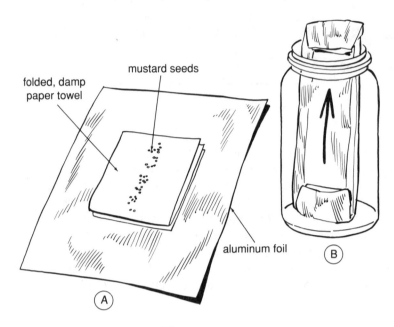

folded, damp
paper towel

mustard seeds

aluminum foil

A

B

Figure 12.1

7. Stand the package in the jar with its arrow pointing upward (see B in Figure 12.1).

8. Place the jar where it can remain undisturbed.

9. After five days, carefully open the package and observe the contents. Make note of the direction of the roots and stems of the seedlings. *Note:* If distinct roots and stems have not yet formed, close the package and reopen it in two days.

Results

The stems of the plants in the package grow up, and the roots grow down.

Why?

Plants are stationary, but they are not motionless. They move slowly, but definitely, in response to stimuli in their environment. This movement in response to a stimulus is called **tropism** and occurs because one part of the plant grows faster than another part. The increased growth is the result of unequal stimulation on opposite sides of the plant.

Auxin is a hormone that causes the cells in a plant to lengthen.

Longer cells on one side cause the plant to bend. Different types of cells respond differently to the presence of this hormone. The increase in length of stem cells is directly related to the concentration of auxin in the cells, whereas auxin inhibits rather than increases the growth of root cells.

The growth response of plants to gravity is called **geotropism.** Gravity pulls the growth-stimulating hormone auxin downward toward the lowest part of the stem and root of a plant. More growth occurs in the cells on the lower side of the stem; less growth in the cells on the lower side of the root. The result is that the stem bends one way, upward, and the roots bend in the opposite direction, downward.

Try New Approaches

1a. Can stems and roots change direction? Repeat the experiment preparing four separate foil packages of seeds. After five days, change the position of the packages to further test the effect of gravity on the stems and roots. Support the jars so that the arrows on the packages point up, down, right, and left (see Figure 12.2). Allow the packages to remain undisturbed for another five days. Open the packages and observe the direction of the stems and roots of each plant. Compare the growth of the stems and roots with the control package (the one with its arrow pointing upward). **Science Fair Hint:** Display a data table with diagrams and descriptions of the seedlings. Record the results by referring to the position of the arrow as up (turned 0°), right (90°), down (180°), and left (270°), as shown in the sample data table here.

Geotropism Data Table	
Plant Direction	Results
up (0°)	
right (90°)	
down (180°)	
left (270°)	

0°   90°

180°   270°

Figure 12.2

b. At what rate do the plants move? Repeat the previous experiment using a clear plastic wrap to cover the seeds. Place the packages inside a dark closet or under a cardboard box to prevent the plants from responding to light. Make as many observations as possible each day. Record the day and time for each observation. Use your results to determine whether there is more plant growth at a specific time of day.

2. Does gravity affect one type of plant more than another? Repeat the original experiment using different types of plant seeds, such as radish, pinto beans, or lima beans. *Note:* Different seeds may require more than five days to germinate. **Science Fair Hint:** Use photographs to represent the procedure and results of the experiment.

Design Your Own Experiment

1. Demonstrate the effect of gravity on mature plants by laying one small houseplant on its side (see A in Figure 12.3). Place a covering or netting over the soil of a second small houseplant to keep it in the pot, and then hang the plant upside down (see B in Figure 12.3). Place both plants inside a dark closet or under a cardboard box to prevent them from responding to light. Observe the position of the stems of each plant after one week. Carefully remove the soil from around the roots of each plant and observe their direction in relationship to the direction of growth of the stems.

2. Does the direction that a seed is planted affect the growth of the stems and roots? Fold a paper towel and line the inside of a drinking glass with it. Stuff pieces of paper towels into the glass to hold the paper lining in place. Place a strip of masking tape around the outside of the glass and mark the tape with arrows pointing up, down, left, and right. Place one pinto bean (between the glass and the paper towel) under each arrow. Make sure the bean's hilum (scar on the inside curved side) is pointing in the direction indicated by the arrow (see Figure 12.4). Moisten the paper towel and keep it moist, but not dripping wet. Place the glass inside a dark closet. Observe the direction of the stems and roots daily for seven days.

Get the Facts

1. How does a plant respond to a low-gravity field as in a spacecraft? Write to NASA (L.B.J. Center, 2101 NASA Rd #1, AP-4, Houston, TX 77058) and request information about growing plants in space.

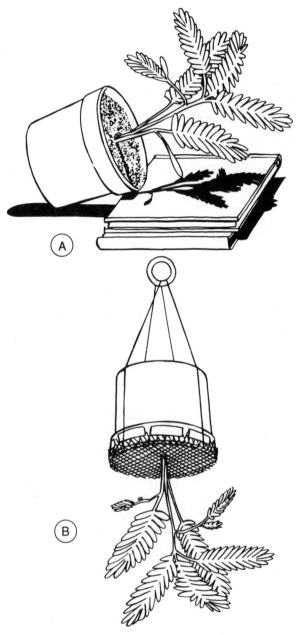

Figure 12.3

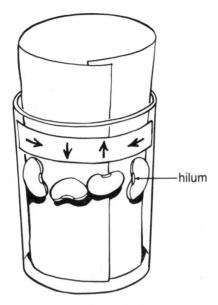

hilum

Figure 12.4

2. How does a simulated-gravity field such as that produced by a rotating space station affect the direction of stem and root growth? A rotating turntable on a record player can produce a simulated field of gravity. More information on growing seeds in this simulated-gravity field can be found in the experiment titled "In or Out?" (p. 50) in Janice Van-Cleave's *Biology for Every Kid* (New York: Wiley, 1990).

Phototropism: Plant Movement Due to Light

13

Plants move in response to light. Phototropism, or plant movement due to light, will be either positive or negative. Positive phototropism is a movement toward light, and negative phototropism is a movement away from light. In this project, you will study the response of plants to light. You will also determine the effect of light intensity and different colors of light on plant movement as well as the rate at which plants move in response to light.

Getting Started

Purpose: To determine the response of oat seedlings to light.

Materials

flowerpot

potting soil

1 tablespoon (15 ml) of oat seeds

water

Procedure

1. Fill the flowerpot with potting soil to within 2 inches (5 cm) from the top.
2. Sprinkle the oat seeds over the surface of the soil.
3. Cover the seeds with about 1 inch (2.5 cm) of soil.
4. Moisten the soil with water and keep it moist, but not dripping wet.
5. Place the pot on a table near a window.
6. Allow the pot to remain undisturbed for 14 days.
7. Make daily observations and record the growth of the oat seeds above the surface of the soil (see Figure 13.1).

Results

The first signs of growth appear in four to six days. Straight, closed tube-like structures break through the soil and grow toward the light. After

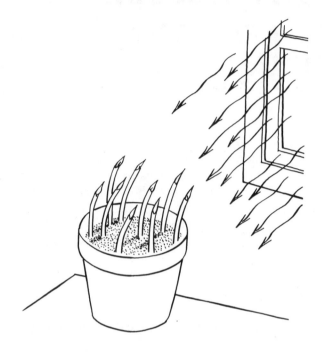

Figure 13.1

several more days, leaves break through the ends of these tubes. The tubes and leaves bend toward the light.

Why?

As the seeds germinate, each primary leaf is protected by a hollow, cylindrical structure, the **coleoptile,** which surrounds it. After the coleoptile has grown above the surface of the soil, it stops growing and the primary leaf breaks through. The coleoptile shoot and the leaf bend toward the light as a result of the buildup of the growth hormone auxin. The auxin migration theory for this **phototropism** (growth toward the light) states that light-sensitive auxin moves from the light side to the dark side of unevenly lighted growing tips. The cells on the shaded side contain a higher concentration of auxin and grow more rapidly than the cells on the lighted side. As a result, the plant bends toward the light.

Try New Approaches

1a. At what rate do the leaves move when seeking light? Place a strip of masking tape around the outside rim of the flowerpot containing the

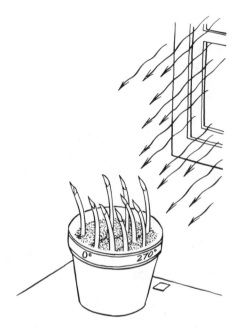

Figure 13.2

oat seedlings. Use a marking pen to mark each quarter point on the circular strip of tape. Start with 0° on the side the seedlings are leaning toward and mark each 90° interval. Place a piece of tape on the table next to the side of the pot facing the window. Use the tape as a reference marker. Turn the pot so that the side marked 180° points to the tape reference marker (see Figure 13.2). The oat leaves should be facing away from the light coming from the window. Record the position of the leaves at four-hour intervals during the daylight periods until the leaves face the window. Record the light conditions for each day. Is it a bright, sunny day? Overcast? Partly cloudy?

b. Is the movement of the leaves toward the light from side to side or do they flip over? Repeat the previous experiment two times, first placing the pot with the leaves facing at an angle or 90° (perpendicular) to the light source, and then having the leaves face 180° (in the opposite direction) to the light source. Observe the position of the leaves at two-hour intervals during the day until the leaves turn toward the light. Make note of the position of the leaves at each observation. To record the changes in the leaves' position, take photo-graphs every two hours. **Science Fair Hint:** Display these time-lapse photographs to indicate the direction of motion of the leaves.

2. Do plants grow toward an artificial light source? Repeat the original experiment placing the oat seedlings in front of a desk lamp. Make sure that the only light source in the room is the incandescent light from the lamp.

3. Charles Darwin and his son Francis discovered that the tip of the coleoptile is necessary for phototropism in oat seedlings. Test this fact for yourself by reproducing their experiment. Repeat the original experiment. When the coleoptiles break through the surface of the soil, use fingernail scissors to snip off the tips of the coleoptiles from half of the seedlings (see Figure 13.3). Position the pot so that plants with and without the tips receive direct sunlight from a window.

Design Your Own Experiment

1a. Do other plants grow toward the light? Experiment by placing differ-ent types of houseplants near a window. Observe the direction of their leaves daily until it is determined that they do or do not respond to light. Use photographs and diagrams to represent the results.

b. Do plants respond to light at different rates? Compare the time it takes for each plant's leaves to respond to the light and measure the degrees that the leaves move. Prepare a graph comparing time and degrees of movement.

2. How do plants respond if two light sources of equal intensity strike them from opposite sides? Place a pot of oat seedlings on a table with two desk lamps 1 foot (30 cm) from either side of the pot. The lamps should be shining directly toward each other with the light rays hit-ting the oat leaves.

3. Test the effect of the color of light by planting a pinto bean in a paper cup filled with moist soil. When the plant growth reaches the rim of the cup, cover it with a second paper cup that has a hole punched in the side (use a pencil to make the hole). Use this cup as the control. Prepare other cups by repeating the procedure, but cover the hole in each cup with a piece of colored cellophane. Prepare as many differ-ent cups as you have colors of cellophane. Raise the top cups covering the plants daily and record each plant's position.

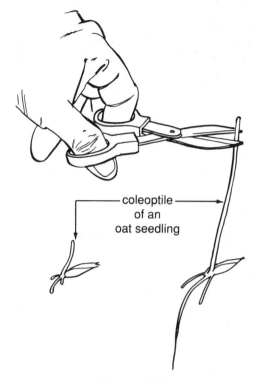

Figure 13.3

Get the Facts

1. The term *auxin* is used to describe any chemical that stimulates elongation of plant cells. Find out more about auxin. How does the concentration of auxin affect cell growth? How is the concentration of auxin controlled? What is polar transport of auxin? What is the acid-growth hypothesis of how auxin causes cell elongation?

2. A plant growing toward a light source exhibits positive phototropism. Roots that grow above ground respond in the opposite manner to light; they exhibit negative phototropism. How does auxin affect the growth of root cells? Use information about root cell response to auxin concentrations to explain the downward growth of roots away from light.

3. Auxin increases the growth of plant cells as a result of light, but how is the light energy actually received by the plant? *Chlorophyll* is a green pigment that receives light energy and uses it in the energy-producing reaction called *photosynthesis*. There are other light-receiving pigments in plant cells. Find out which light waves the phototropic response is most sensitive to and the pigment that is most likely to receive this light energy.

Photomorphogenesis: Plant Responses to Light

14

Photomorphogenesis involves plant responses initiated by light stimuli that are not from a specific direction or applied for any particular time period. An example of photomorphogenesis is etiolation, the elongation of plant stems caused by the absence of light.

In this project, you will have the opportunity to learn about the effect of light on the formation of plant tissues. The effects of the quantity and quality of light on etiolation will be determined. You will also look at the effects of light filtered by solar window film and of colored light on etiolation.

Getting Started

Purpose: To determine the effect of light on plant stem elongation.

Materials

2 7-ounce (210-ml) paper cups	8 pinto beans
potting soil	water
pencil	cardboard box about 18 inches
2 saucers	(45 cm) tall
	masking tape

Procedure

1. Fill each paper cup with potting soil to within 1 inch (2.5 cm) from the top.
2. Use the pencil to punch two holes into either side near the bottom of each cup.
3. Set the cups in separate saucers.
4. Plant four beans about 1 inch (2.5 cm) deep in each cup of soil.
5. Moisten the soil in each cup with water and keep it moist during the entire experiment.

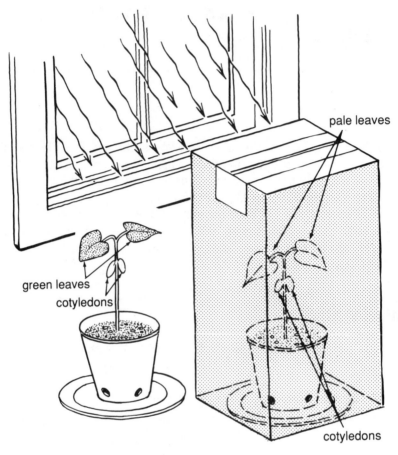

green leaves

cotyledons

pale leaves

cotyledons

Figure 14.1

6. Place the cups together near a window.

7. Put one cup inside the cardboard box. Seal all cracks in the box with the masking tape to prevent light from entering. *Note:* To add water to the plants inside the box, open the box inside a dark closet and seal the box before leaving the closet.

8. At the end of two weeks, open the box and compare the length, diameter, and color of the stems of the plants grown with and without light (see Figure 14.1).

Results

The plants grown in darkness have a spindly appearance. Their stems are longer, smaller in diameter, and paler in color compared to the short, sturdy, green stems of the plants grown in light. The development of the leaves of the plants grown in darkness is slower than that of the plants grown in light.

Why?

Photomorphogenesis is the term used to denote plant responses to light stimuli that are not specifically directional or periodic. The elongation of the stems of the plants grown in darkness is the result of a type of photomorphogenesis known as **etiolation.** The excessive lengthening of the cells in each stem is caused by the abnormally high levels of auxin and ethylene (growth-regulating hormones in plants).

The paleness of the stems of the dark-grown plants is a result of the lack of chloroplasts. **Chloroplasts** are cell structures that develop from small, colorless cell structures called proplastids. In the presence of light, the colorless proplastids develop into green chloroplasts. The green color is a result of the development, within the chloroplasts, of a green color pigment—chlorophyll. **Chlorophyll** is a light-sensitive molecule necessary to accomplish photosynthesis (light-stimulated, energy-producing reaction in plants). In the absence of light, the proplastids do not develop into chloroplasts, which results in the plants' pale color.

Light also affects the production of different kinds of growth hormones in the cells of the plants grown in sunlight. Low levels of these hormones cause the cells to be less elongated. Thus, plants grown with light have short, thick stems compared to the stems of plants grown without light.

Try New Approaches

1a. How much light is needed to prevent etiolation? Repeat the experiment cutting a 2-inch (5-cm) diameter hole in the side of the box. Cover the hole with a piece of opaque paper (see Figure 14.2). At the same time each day during the test period, lift the paper cover from the hole and allow light to enter the box for five minutes. Close the cover and secure it with masking tape to prevent any extra light from entering. *Note:* Further testing of the quantity of light needed to inhibit etiolation can be done by using larger or smaller holes in the box and by increasing or decreasing the amount of time the light enters the box.

b. Does the type of light affect the results? Repeat the experiment using

Figure 14.2

different light sources, such as a fluorescent light, incandescent bulbs, and/or plant grow-lights.

2a. How does solar window film affect plant growth? Repeat the preceding experiment covering the hole in the box with a piece of solar window film. (For a list of companies who sell solar window film, look under "Glass Coating and Tinting" in your telephone directory.)

b. Does the color of the light affect etiolation? Repeat the experiment using different colors of cellophane to cover the hole in the box. **Science Fair Hint:** Use photographs to represent the procedure and results of the experiment.

Design Your Own Experiment

1. Can etiolation occur in the light? Test the effect of ethylene—a gas released by ripening fruit that affects plant growth—on plant cell elongation by placing two bean seedlings, one each, inside two large glass jars. Add a piece of ripened fruit, such as a banana, to one of the jars. Secure the lids on the jars and place them near a window where they will receive equal amounts of light. Observe the growth of the plants for one week. Find out more about the effect of ethylene on plant growth and include these facts along with the results of the experiment in your project summary.

2a. Another way to demonstrate etiolation is to grow bean seeds inside a closed aluminum foil package. Prepare a package by placing six or eight pinto or lima beans on a paper towel. Roll the towel around the beans and place the roll in the center of a piece of aluminum foil. Moisten the paper towel with water. Fold the foil around the paper roll and close up each end of the foil. After ten days, open the package and observe the stems of the seedlings.

b. Design ways of using the foil packages containing beans to test the effect of the quantity of light on etiolation. One way might be to punch holes in the aluminum foil to allow a specific amount of light to enter each package.

Get the Facts

1. Many types of seed remain more or less dormant if kept completely in the dark, but light inhibits the germination of other seeds. Find out more about the effect of light on seed germination. Which wavelengths of light are most effective in promoting germination? Which wavelength of light inhibits seed germination? What role does *phytochrome* (a light-absorbing pigment) play in the effect that different light waves have on seed germination?

2. The response of any organism to light is mediated by *light-sensitive pigments* (molecules that change when they absorb light). Many plants respond to changes in the *photoperiod* (period of daylight) by making physiological changes such as the formation of flowers. How do pigments affect the ability of plants to respond to photoperiods? Learn more about photoperiodic control of plants. Discover the biochemistry behind plants' seeming ability to tell time. What is the critical photoperiod? Give examples and differences between short-day, long-day, and day-neutral plants.

The energy-producing reaction of photosynthesis occurs in leaves. This reaction requires that a large and steady supply of carbon dioxide gas be brought into the leaf. It also produces an equal amount of oxygen gas that must be released from the leaf. The regulation of this exchange of gases occurs through special openings, or stomata, in the leaf.

In this project, you will determine the position of stomata and the effect of the environment on the stomata. You will also look at the mechanism of the opening and closing of the stomata as well as factors affecting this mechanism.

Getting Started

Purpose: To demonstrate that leaves have openings through which gases can enter.

Materials

small glass soda bottle	modeling clay
water	pencil
knife	flexible drinking straw
ivy leaf with stem	mirror

Procedure

1. Fill the soda bottle with water to within 1 inch (2.5 cm) from the top.
2. Use the knife to make a diagonal cut across the end of the stem of the ivy.
3. Wrap a roll of clay around the stem near the leaf.
4. Place the stem into the bottle with its end below the surface of the water.
5. Cover the mouth of the bottle with the clay.
6. Push the pencil through the clay to make an opening for the straw.
7. Insert the straw so that its opening is in the air space at the top of the bottle.

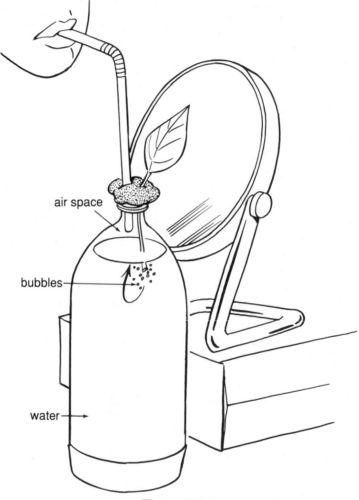

air space

bubbles

water

Figure 15.1

8. Squeeze the clay around the straw to close off the opening of the bottle, being careful not to flatten the straw.

9. Stand in front of the mirror and look at the mirror image of the end of the stem while you suck the air out of the bottle through the straw (see Figure 15.1). This should be difficult if there are no leaks in the clay, so use a lot of suction.

Results

Bubbles form in the water at the cut end of the bottom of the ivy stem.

Why?

Stomata are special openings in the epidermis of a leaf through which gases pass. Xylem vessels are thick-walled, hollow, cylindrical tubes that run throughout the leaf and down the stem and transport water and minerals from the roots to the leaf. In this experiment, the leaf and stem of the ivy are forced to act like a straw, which shows that leaves do have holes (stomata) through which gasses can pass.

The air is forced through the leaf because of a difference in air pressure inside and outside the bottle. Sucking the air out of the bottle lowers the air pressure inside the bottle. The higher air pressure outside the bottle then pushes air into the leaf through the stomata, down through the xylem, and out the open end of the stem, forming bubbles in the water.

Try New Approaches

1. Are more stomata found on the front or back of a leaf? Repeat the experiment two times, first placing a thick coating of petroleum jelly on the back of the ivy leaf, and then placing a thick coating of petroleum jelly on the front of the leaf. **Science Fair Hint:** Display a photograph of someone using the leaf straw. Next to the photograph, display two diagrams—one showing petroleum jelly on the top of a leaf and the other showing petroleum jelly on the bottom of a leaf. Indicate which leaf allows air to pass through by showing bubbles in the water beneath the stem.

2. Do other plant leaves have stomata? Repeat the original experiment using a stem and leaf from other houseplants or try a stalk of celery with its leaves attached.

CAUTION: Check with a plant nursery professional to select nontoxic plants.

Design Your Own Experiment

1a. Does the density of stomata vary in different areas of a leaf? Prepare a wet-mount slide of the thin, transparent, lower epidermal layer of a

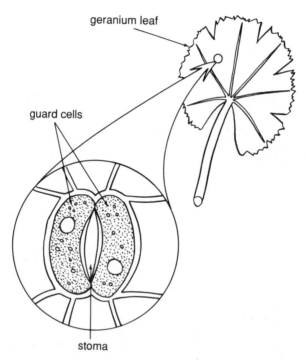

geranium leaf

guard cells

stoma

Figure 15.2

geranium leaf. See Appendix 1 for instructions on preparing slides. Separate the transparent epidermal layer from the leaf by laying a freshly picked leaf, front side up, on a sheet of paper. Gently scrape the edge of a single-edge razor blade back and forth across the front side of the leaf to remove all the colored layers. Handling the razor carefully, cut off a small section of the transparent layer and immediately place it and a drop of water on a microscope slide. Position a coverslip over it. Do not allow the tissue to dry out. Look for small bean-shaped structures under low power. The bean-shaped structures are guard cells, and the opening visible between the guard cells is the stoma (see Figure 15.2). Count the visible stomata in one low-power field. Repeat the experiment to prepare slides from different sections of the leaf. Make drawings and, if photographic attachments for the microscope are available, take pictures of each slide.

b. Examine the slides under high power to get a better view of the difference in thickness of the walls of the guard cells.

2a. Guard cells regulate the movement of water vapor and gases into and out of the leaf. How do the guard cells respond to great amounts of water loss? Prepare a fresh wet-mount slide of the transparent epidermis of a leaf. Place a drop of table salt solution [1 teaspoon [5 ml] salt in 1 cup (250 ml) of water] at the edge of the coverslip. Touch the opposite edge of the coverslip with a paper towel so that you draw the salty water under the coverslip and bathe the epidermis sample. Wait about five minutes and observe the guard cells under the high power. Make drawings of the microscopic observations. Use the diagrams for the displays and as part of the project report. Reference these drawings and/or photographs when giving an oral presentation.

b. Repeat the experiment with leaves from different plants. Make several slides and compare and note any differences in the appearance of the stomata.

Get the Facts

1. Specialized cells called *guard cells* surround each stoma in a leaf. Stomata are fully open during daylight and closed during the night. Find out how the guard cells regulate the opening and closing of the stomata. Of what benefit is it to the plant for the stomata to be closed?

2. When stomata are open, oxygen and water vapor move out of the leaves and carbon dioxide moves in. Find out more about the exchange of gases in a plant. By what method do the gases enter and exit cells? What regulates the leaving of one type of gas and at the same time the entrance of another type of gas? Does water vapor always leave the cells when the stomata are open? What keeps cells from losing too much water?

3. Water content of guard cells affects their shape and thus changes the size of the stoma opening. Find out more about the movement of water into and out of a cell. What is a concentration gradient? How does it affect the loss and gain of water in a cell? What is osmosis? How do temperature and humidity affect the exchange of water from a cell?

4. Air pollutants often coat the leaves of plants. Find out more about the effect of pollution on plants. What happens when the coating of pollution is thick enough to close off the stomata?

16 Photosynthesis and Respiration

For survival, plants as well as animals need the energy stored in chemical bonds. By photosynthesis, plants convert the energy from the sun into chemical energy stored in the form of complex sugar molecules. By respiration, plants release this stored chemical energy.

In this project, you will examine the processes of photosynthesis and respiration and determine substances consumed and produced in each. You will also look at factors affecting these reactions, such as light and the presence of oxygen.

Getting Started

Purpose: To determine whether respiration goes on in plant tissue.

Materials

3 baby food jars with lids

distilled water

marking pen

2 sprigs of elodea or other water plant (found at a pet store)

brom thymol blue indicator (see Appendix 2)

1-×-1-foot (30-×-30-cm) sheet of aluminum foil

desk lamp

Procedure

1. Rinse the baby food jars with distilled water.

2. Use the marking pen to number the jars 1, 2, and 3.

3. Place a sprig of elodea into jars 1 and 2.

4. Fill all three jars with brom thymol blue indicator.

5. Put the lid on each jar.

6. Cover jar 1 with the aluminum foil so that no light can enter.

7. Place all three jars about 8 inches (20 cm) in front of the desk lamp (see Figure 16.1).

8. Check the color of the solution in each jar every hour for eight hours. Take care to quickly replace the aluminum foil over jar 1.

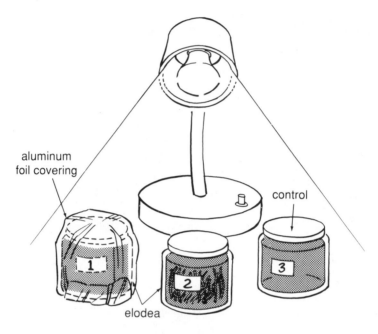

Figure 16.1

Results

The color of the solution in jar 1 changes from blue to green and finally to yellow. The changes in jar 1 occur quickly. The color of the solution in jar 2 slowly turns green. The color of the solution in jar 3 remains unchanged.

Why?

Brom thymol blue indicator contains water and a dye extract. This indicator can be used to test for the presence of carbon dioxide. When carbon dioxide combines with water, it forms a weak acid (carbonic acid). Depending on the amount of carbon dioxide dissolved, the indicator turns from blue to green or yellow (the more carbon dioxide, the more yellow the liquid turns).

Photosynthesis and respiration are the two energy-producing reactions in plants. Photosynthesis requires light and occurs only during the day. Respiration goes on day and night. These reactions are exact opposites of each other: **Respiration** combines sugar and oxygen to form carbon dioxide and water; photosynthesis, with energy from light, combines carbon dioxide and water to form sugar and oxygen.

In the dark, the plant in jar 1 produces energy by respiration. A large amount of carbon dioxide is released, as indicated by the changing of the solution from blue to yellow. Both photosynthesis and respiration occur in jar 2. Carbon dioxide is produced by the plant during the respiration reaction, but some of it is removed from the solution during the photosynthesis reaction. The green color of the solution indicates the presence of a smaller concentration of carbon dioxide. Jar 3 is the control. Without plants, neither photosynthesis nor respiration can occur in the jar, so the color of the brom thymol blue remains unchanged.

Try New Approaches

1. Does the amount of light affect the results? Repeat the experiment two times, first placing the jars closer to the light source and then placing them farther away.

2. Does the source of light affect the results? Repeat the original experiment using various light sources, such as sunlight, incandescent bulbs, fluorescent lighting, and plant grow-lights. Compare the results.

3. How do different colors of light affect the results? Repeat the original experiment several times, and with each test cover the jars with a different color of cellophane.

Design Your Own Experiment

1. Respiration in animals and plants is generally the same. Gases are exchanged between the atmosphere and the bodies of the organisms. Check for the presence of carbon dioxide in your exhaled breath by breathing through a drinking straw into a small glass soda bottle half filled with a solution of brom thymol blue indicator. Count the number of exhaled breaths needed to produce a yellow color. Repeat the experiment two times, first after sitting and resting for five minutes, and then after exercise (such as climbing stairs) for one minute. Prepare a bar graph to compare the results.

CAUTION: Perform the exercise section only if your health permits such an activity.

2. Seeds do not need light to germinate. Find out whether germinating seeds release carbon dioxide and thus produce energy by respiration. Fill a small glass soda bottle one-third full with pinto beans and pour

Figure 16.2

water over the beans. Let the beans soak overnight and then pour off the water. Insert the end of a flexible drinking straw into the mouth of the bottle. Use modeling clay to secure the straw and close off the bottle. Insert the free end of the straw into a glass of brom thymol blue indicator (see Figure 16.2). Observe the color of the solution to determine whether carbon dioxide is present.

3. **Aerobic** means "in the presence of oxygen." Anaerobic means without the presence of oxygen. In aerobic respiration, the products of respiration are glucose, carbon dioxide, and energy. In anaerobic respiration, the products are alcohol, carbon dioxide, and energy. **Fermentation** is anaerobic respiration. Use yeast to demonstrate fermentation and brom thymol blue indicator to test for the presence of carbon dioxide. Fill a glass soda bottle half full with warm water. Add ¼ ounce (7 g) of dry yeast and 3 tablespoons (45 ml) of sugar. Insert the end of a flexible drinking straw into the mouth of the bottle above the liquid level. Use modeling clay to seal the mouth of the bottle around the straw. Insert the free end of the straw into a glass filled with brom thymol blue.

4. Plants live for long periods of time in terrariums. This ability to live in closed containers without outside supplies is due to the fact that plants carry on two balanced energy-producing processes—photosynthesis and respiration. Find out from a plant nursery professional what is needed to construct a terrarium and build one. Use the terrarium as part of your display if a plastic container is used (for safety, glass containers are usually not allowed in most science fairs). Next to the terrarium, display the equations for the two energy reactions to show that the products of one reaction are the raw materials needed for the second reaction.

Get the Facts

1. Gases enter and leave plants through openings in the leaves called *stomata* and through openings in the stem called *lenticels*. You breathe in and exhale out through your nose and mouth, but earthworms absorb and release gases through their moist skin. Find out how other organisms exchange gases in order for respiration to occur.

2. Respiration is a cellular activity. Where inside the cell does this reaction occur? How does the cell store and release the energy produced by respiration?

3. Find out more about fermentation. What is the purpose of yeast? How can winemakers assure that alcohol and not acid is the product of the fermentation of their grapes?

17 Chromatography: Solar Photography

Plant parts are of various colors depending on the type and amount of color pigment they contain. Leaves get their green color from a light-sensitive substance found in special plant cells, or chloroplasts.

In this project, you will determine how the color pigment found in plant leaves is affected by sunlight. The pigment will be separated for identification by a process called chromatography—separating solid components of a mixture by their differential absorption as they pass through an absorbing material. You will also study the effect that color pigments have on a plant.

Getting Started

Purpose: To determine the effect of sunlight on the color of leaves.

Materials

scissors

black construction paper

geranium plant

masking tape

Procedure

1. Use scissors to cut two sections from the black construction paper that are large enough to cover one leaf on the geranium plant. *Note:* The paper pieces should be slightly larger than a leaf on the plant.
2. Cut out a heart-shaped piece from the center of one of the paper pieces and save the outline (not the heart).
3. Sandwich a leaf between the two paper pieces, being very careful not to damage the leaf.
4. Tape the paper pieces together along their edges (see Figure 17.1).
5. Repeat the procedure attaching papers with heart-shaped cutouts on three or four leaves.
6. Place the plant in a sunny area.
7. Wait seven days.

Figure 17.1

8. Carefully remove the papers without damaging the leaves.

9. Observe the areas of the leaves that were covered by the papers.

Results

In areas covered by the black paper, the leaves change from dark green to pale green, yellow, or even white. There is a dark green heart where the leaf was exposed to light.

Why?

A chemical called chlorophyll (chloro = green and phyll = leaf) gives leaves their green color. Chlorophyll is found in special plant cells, or chloroplasts (site where the energy-producing reaction of photosynthesis occurs). Light is necessary for the development of chlorophyll.

Before a germinating seed breaks through the surface of the soil to receive light, the parts of the developing plant are pale. Colorless structures called **proplastids** are present. The presence of light changes proplastids to green chloroplasts. In the absence of light the leaf changes from dark green to a paler color as chloroplasts change to colorless **plastids** (organelles formed from proplastids that usually contain pigments, but some are colorless).

The opaque paper blocks the sun's light; thus, in the covered areas, the chloroplasts change to colorless plastids. Light shines through the cutout sections; thus, the chloroplasts remain a dark green.

Try New Approaches

1. How long does it take for the green chloroplasts to change? An exact time for the conversion of one structure of chloroplast cannot be determined with this experiment, but a general time can be determined from observing color changes during a measured time period. Repeat the experiment using enough plants to provide 14 healthy leaves. Cover the 14 leaves with solid pieces of black construction paper instead of using pieces with heart shapes cut from their centers. Prepare the leaves at night so that you can begin the experiment with the rising of the sun on the first day. Remove one paper patch after the covered leaf has received one-half of the light scheduled for that day. Take a color photograph to obtain the best record of the leaf's color. Remove the second paper patch at the end of the first day and photograph the leaf again. Continue this schedule of removing the patches. Compare the photographs to determine the time required to make a noticeable color change in the leaves. *Note:* Light duration and intensity vary with seasons. If possible, repeat the experiment during different seasons and compare the results. Make note of the season in which you perform the experiment.

2. Do the faded areas of a leaf return to their original green color if exposed to light? Use any of the plants that have faded leaves produced by covering the leaves with opaque paper. Place the plants where they will receive light. Watch them daily for seven days and use photographs to record any daily color changes. **Science Fair Hint:** Use the photographs to represent procedures and results.

3. Is light energy received on all of a leaf's surfaces? Repeat the original experiment covering different leaves in three different ways: front and back, only the front, and only the back.

Design Your Own Experiment

1. Is chlorophyll the only color pigment in a leaf? Make a dark green mark about 1 inch (2.5 cm) from the rounded edge of a paper coffee filter by placing a leaf, top side down, on the paper and rubbing the edge of a coin back and forth over the leaf. Allow the green mark on the paper to dry before repeating the process. You want to collect enough pigment from the leaf to make a dark green line on the paper. Fold the paper filter in half twice and secure with a paper clip to form a cone. Pour a small amount of rubbing alcohol into a saucer.

CAUTION: Keep the alcohol away from your nose and mouth.

Place the rounded edge of the paper cone into the alcohol. To prevent the alcohol from evaporating too quickly, cover the paper and saucer with a 2-liter plastic soda bottle that has a cap and its bottom cut away (see Figure 17.2). Allow the paper to sit undisturbed for 30 minutes. Study any colored streaks on the paper and identify the pigments:

- carotene—orange
- xanthophyll—yellow
- chlorophyll (a)—blue-green
- chlorophyll (b)—yellow-green
- anthocyanin—red

2a. What makes a red apple red? The red color of an apple is from the color pigment anthocyanin. Other plant pigments are located in plastids, but anthocyanins are found in cell sap. Anthocyanin is red in the acid solution of the cell sap, giving the skin of the apple a red color. Anthocyanin can be separated by boiling the peeling from a red apple in 1 cup (250 ml) of distilled water. The resulting pale color of the cooked peeling and water is due to the neutralization of the acidic cell sap by the basic content of the ruptured cells. Add vinegar (an acid) to the liquid in which the apple skin is boiled to test for the presence of anthocyanin.

b. Would the color of anthocyanin be affected differently if the cell sap was alkaline? Test the effects of an alkaline on the color of anthocyanin by adding drops of household ammonia or limewater to the liquid that the peel of a red apple has been boiled in. See Appendix 2 for instructions on making limewater.

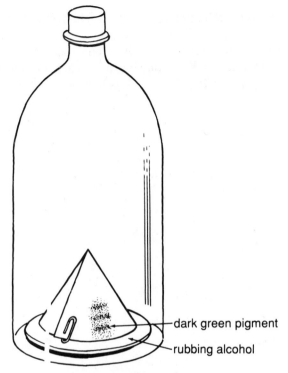

dark green pigment

rubbing alcohol

Figure 17.2

CAUTION: Ammonia is a poison. It and its fumes can damage skin and mucous membranes of nose, mouth, and eyes.

Get the Facts

1. Chlorophyll produces the green color in plants, but other colored pigments also exist in green leaves. Find out more about plant color pigments. What causes the brilliant color changes in leaves during the fall? What environmental conditions produce the most colorful leaves? What is the pigment's function other than producing color?

2. Minor changes in a chemical formula can make major changes in the physical and chemical properties of a substance. Chlorophyll and hemoglobin are amazingly alike. Both contain 137 atoms. A replacement of one atom could change hemoglobin to chlorophyll and vice versa. Find out more about chlorophyll and hemoglobin. How do the two molecules compare structurally? Draw and display a structural diagram for comparison. What function does each play in the energy-producing reactions with which each is involved?

PART II

Zoology

Responses of Annelidas: Segmented Worms

Segmented worms such as the earthworm belong to the phylum Annelida. These worms have a more advanced body structure than most worms. The body of the earthworm is like two tubes, one inside used for digesting food and one outside serving as the body wall. The earthworm has a mouth but no nose, eyes, or ears. Yet it responds to odors and to changes in moisture, temperature, and light.

In this project, you will have the opportunity to unravel these paradoxes by observing and testing an earthworm's responses to various stimuli. You will also test the learning ability of earthworms. *Note:* No earthworms should die from any of the experiments in this project. Handle the worms with care. At the conclusion of the project, place the worms outside in a shady area of soil.

Getting Started

Purpose: To observe an earthworm in a simulated (near-natural) soil environment.

Materials

3 cups (750 ml) of potting soil

1-quart (1-liter) glass jar with lid

1 cup (250 ml) of water

8 to 10 earthworms (from a bait shop, or dig your own)

apple peelings

sheet of newspaper

rubber bands

hammer

large nail

Procedure

1. Pour the soil into the jar.

2. Moisten the soil with water and keep it moist during the entire project.

3. Put the worms into the jar.

115

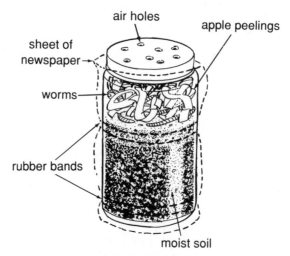

Figure 18.1

4. Place the apple peelings on the surface of the soil and keep the worms supplied with peelings during the entire project.

5. Fold the newspaper so that it fits around the outside of the jar. Secure it with the rubber bands.

6. Use the hammer and nail to make five or six holes in the lid of the jar.

7. Secure the lid and place the jar in a cool place (see Figure 18.1).

8. Remove the paper and observe the jar every day for two weeks.

Results

The worms start wiggling immediately and burrow into the soil. A network of tunnels can be seen in the soil. The apple peelings disappear, and **casts** (undigested soil deposits) appear on the surface of the soil.

Why?

Earthworms spend their lives in one small area of the ground. In some places there are 50,000 worms per acre of soil. An earthworm's diet consists of the animal and vegetable matter in the soil, which is pulled into the worm's mouth by muscles in its body. Nutrients are extracted as the soil passes through the earthworm's digestive tube and out the other end. In this way, earthworms are very beneficial because their tunneling and digestive process loosens and aerates the soil.

Try New Approaches

1. How does low temperature affect the activity of the worms? Place the jar of worms in a refrigerator. Make daily observations of the movement of the worms inside the jar for one week. Keep the worms in the refrigerator for the remainder of the project. The body temperature of worms changes with their environment. Their metabolism is reduced in cold temperatures, so they become more lethargic. Thus, more worms can be contained in a smaller area for longer periods of time.

Design Your Own Experiment

1. Which end of the earthworm is more sensitive to odor? Moisten a paper towel and lay it on a table. Place one worm on it. Wet a cotton ball with fingernail polish remover. Hold the wet cotton ball near, but not touching, the anterior end (the more pointed and darker end) of each worm. Repeat at the posterior end (rear end) and at segments between the ends.

2. Does the earthworm prefer wet or dry surfaces? Lay two pieces of wet and dry paper towels next to each other, but not touching, on a table. Place an earthworm across the two surfaces, anterior end on the wet towel, and observe the response. Then reverse the worm's position so that the anterior end is on the dry towel. Again, observe the response.

3a. Does the earthworm respond faster at a higher or a lower body temperature? Prepare two containers of worms by placing soil and three worms in two separate baby food jars. Place one jar in a refrigerator and keep the other at room temperature. After 24 hours, use the worms from each jar to test their response to odor and preference for wet or dry paper.

b. Use a stereomicroscope (dissecting microscope) to measure the change in heart rate of the worms at different body temperatures. Place one worm at a time under the microscope. Find the earthworm's dorsal aorta (the blood vessel running along the uppermost region of the back). You should see a wavelike contraction moving from the posterior end to the anterior end. Each wave is a single "heartbeat." Count the beats in one minute. Measure the temperature of the soil. Make additional temperature changes by sitting the containers in a bowl of ice water. Do not heat the water because you will

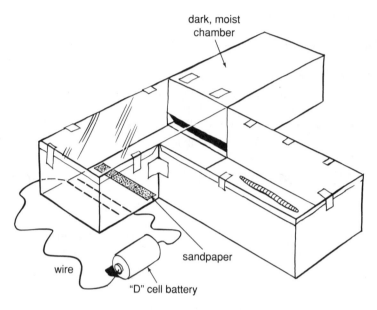

dark, moist
chamber

sandpaper

wire

"D" cell battery

Figure 18.2

injure the worms. Prepare a graph using temperature as the independent variable (x-axis) and heartbeat as the dependent variable (y-axis).

4. Can an earthworm learn simple, consistent choices when confronted with alternatives? Use shoe boxes to construct a T-maze (see Figure 18.2). Cover the top with several layers of red cellophane and restrict direct light on the maze. Use a "D" cell battery and wire to supply a brief electric shock when the worm touches the wire. Earthworms can learn to take the arm of the maze leading to the reward (darkness and moisture) and away from the punishment (light, dryness, sandpaper, and electric shock). The development of this response is slow and will require many trials. Separate the worms that are learning the maze and place them in their own container. It is thought that earthworms can learn to make the correct choice 90% of the time. How well do your worms learn? How long do they retain what they learn? Display the maze and photographs showing the worms during a typical learning lesson as well as a graph comparing the trials for each worm in training.

Get the Facts

1. The American earthworm belongs to the genus *Lumbricus.* Charles Darwin first showed that this worm is important because it aerates the soil by digging tunnels and aids in the growth of plants by dragging seeds from the surface into the damp soil where they can germinate. Use an encyclopedia to find out more about the benefits of earthworms. How deep do they tunnel? How much soil do they bring to the surface annually?

2. Earthworms have a nervous system but no obvious sense organs such as eyes. But the worms do respond to light stimuli. How? Use a biology text to find information about the sensory responses of worms. Also read the experiment titled "Night Crawlers" (pp. 124–125) in Janice VanCleave's *Biology for Every Kid* (New York: Wiley, 1990).

19 Conditions Affecting Bacterial Growth

Bacteria can be found everywhere. A single bacterium cannot be seen but, if provided with the right conditions, will multiply into a visible colony, or group, of bacteria cells.

In this project, you will provide a nutritious diet for bacteria so that they can be grown for observation. The semisterile conditions of this project will allow you to test the effect of temperature, light, and disinfectants on bacterial growth.

Getting Started

Purpose: To determine how to culture bacterial growths.

Materials

24 small baby food jars with lids	1-cup (250-ml) distilled water
dishwashing liquid	spoon
water	1 beef bouillon cube
paper towels	cookie sheet
knife	oven
small potato weighing about 6 ounces (170 g)	marking pen
	masking tape
small saucepan	soap
stove	
0.25 ounce (7 g) of unflavored gelatin	

Procedure

1. Wash the jars and lids with dishwashing liquid and rinse with water. Turn them upside down on paper towels to drain.
2. Use the knife to peel and cut the potato into small pieces.
3. Place the potato pieces into the saucepan with 2 cups (500 ml) of water.

4. Place the saucepan on the stove and boil the potato pieces until they are well done. Drain them and save the liquid potato broth.

5. Sprinkle the gelatin over the surface of 1 cup (250 ml) of distilled water. Allow to stand for two minutes and then stir.

6. Add the gelatin and bouillon cube to the potato broth in the saucepan.

7. Cook over medium heat, stirring constantly, until the bouillon cube and all of the gelatin dissolve.

8. Pour the hot gelatin mixture into the four jars in equal amounts.

9. Quickly secure the lids on each jar.

10. Place the jars on the cookie sheet and bake them in the oven at 250°F (121°C) for one hour.

11. Allow the jars to cool before removing them from the oven. Place 20 jars in a refrigerator for use in later experiments.

12. Allow the gelatin to congeal in the remaining four jars, then lift the lid of one jar. Keep the lid over the jar as you press several of your fingertips, one at a time, against the gelatin. Do not cut into the gel.

13. Secure the lid on the jar. Use the marking pen and masking tape to number the jar 1 and label it "Fingertips."

14. Wash your hands with soap and dry them with the paper towels.

15. Rub your fingertips across a well-traveled area of a tile floor.

16. Lift the lid of the second jar and press several fingertips against the gelatin. Secure the lid. Number the jar 2 and label it "Floor."

17. Repeat the procedure (steps 14 through 16) to collect a sample from a doorknob. Number this jar 3 and label it "Doorknob."

18. Do not open the last jar. Label it 4 and "Control."

19. Place the jars in a dark, warm place, such as a closet containing a water heater, for two to four days (see Figure 19.1).

Results

Spots of growth can be seen on all of the test surfaces except that of the control jar. If growths are seen in the control jar, prepare new jars, bake the jars for a longer time period, and then repeat the experiment.

Why?

Bacteria are very small, one-celled, microscopic organisms that are found in air, water, soil, and the bodies of other living organisms. The

culture medium = potato broth + distilled water + gelatin + boullion

Figure 19.1

gelatin provides a **culture medium** (specially prepared nutritious substance) on which bacteria grow into a visible **colony** (group of cells). Baking the jars kills any pre-existing bacteria. The placement of samples of material onto the culture medium is called **inoculation.** The lid is held above each jar during inoculation to prevent particles from the air from falling into the container.

Try New Approaches

1. How does temperature affect bacterial growth? Repeat the experiment making two samples of each of the three inoculations. Add "Warm" and "Cold" to the labels. Place the warm samples in a dark, warm place (such as the water heater closet) and the cold samples in a dark, cool place (such as a refrigerator).

2. Do bacteria grow better where it is light or dark? Repeat the original experiment making two samples of each of the three inoculations. Add "Light" and "Dark" to the labels. Place the light samples in a warm place where an electric bulb can shine on them all the time. Be sure that the bulb is not so close that it changes the temperature of the jars. Place the dark samples in a dark, warm place.

3. Is deodorant soap more **bactericidal** (able to kill bacteria) than pure soap? Repeat the original experiment making two samples from each of the three testing surfaces. Rub your hands across one of the surfaces and ask a helper to wash one of your hands with deodorant soap before making one inoculation. Have your second hand washed with pure soap before making the second set. Repeat the procedure for each testing surface.

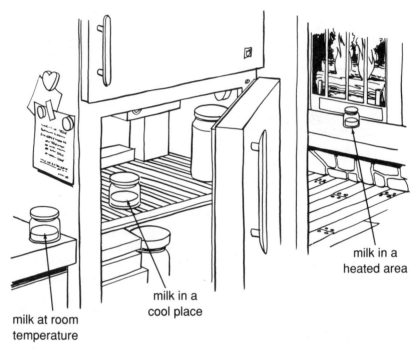

milk in a
heated area

milk in a
cool place

milk at room
temperature

Figure 19.2

4. Which deodorant soap is the most bactericidal? Repeat the preceding experiment using different brands of deodorant soap. **Science Fair Hint:** Triclocarban is an antibacterial agent that inhibits the growth of bacteria. Discover whether all deodorant products contain triclocarban by checking the labels on different deodorant soap and antiperspirant products. Make and display a list of the active ingredients in each product.

5. Do disinfectants kill bacteria? Repeat the original experiment inoculating as many culture jars as you have samples of disinfectants. Rinse the surface of each gel with a different disinfectant after each inoculation. Use two controls—one with no inoculation and the other with no inoculation but rinsed with distilled water. **Science Fair Hint:** Since culture jars are usually not allowed to be displayed for safety reasons, display sample jars without the bacterial cultures. Take photographs of the jars and their contents as the experiment progresses to represent the procedure and results.

Design Your Own Experiment

1. Warm temperatures promote the growth of bacteria that can cause food to spoil. Milk contains some bacteria and will eventually spoil even when refrigerated. Determine how long it takes milk to spoil at different temperatures. Place closed containers of milk in areas of different temperatures, such as at room temperature, in a refrigerator, and near a heater or fireplace (see Figure 19.2). Spoilage of milk is evident by the presence of thick, white lumps and a sour smell.

CAUTION: Do not taste the milk used in this experiment. It could make you sick.

2. Are there bacteria in the air? Repeat the preceding experiment using different containers of milk but leaving the jars uncovered. Compare the time required for the milk to spoil in an open container and a closed container. **Science Fair Hint:** Display graphs of your results.

Get the Facts

1. Most bacteria are harmless. Many are even beneficial. Find out more about bacteria. What is the difference between and what are some examples of saprophytic, pathogenic, and nonpathogenic bacteria? What are some of the ways in which bacteria are beneficial? What diseases are caused by bacteria? What are nitrogen-fixing bacteria and how are they important to soil fertility? What would the world be like if there were no bacteria? You could use the answers in a project report. You could also prepare a data table for display showing diagrams of and listing the human diseases caused by the three major morphological types of bacteria:
   - bacilli—rod-shaped
   - cocci—round
   - spirilla—spiral-shaped

   (See the sample data table in Figure 19.3.)

2. Antiseptics and disinfectants are used to control the growth of bacteria and to prevent infections. These chemicals cannot be used to treat

Bacteria Types and Diseases They Cause

Bacilli	Cocci	Spirilla
		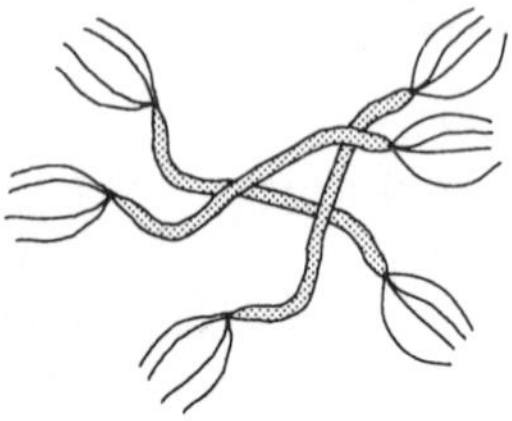
leprosy tetanus diphtheria	Note: Fill in other diseases here.	

Figure 19.3

internal body infections. Other chemicals called *antibiotics* are used to control bacterial growths inside the bodies of animals. Find out more about these special life-saving "miracle drugs." How long have they been used? What was the first antibiotic used, who discovered it, and how was it discovered?

20 Food Preservatives

In our complex world, food products have to be shipped for long distances and/or stored for periods of time. It would be difficult to transport and store most kinds of food without using preservative additives.

In this project, you will have the opportunity to test the effectiveness of calcium propionate, a food additive that inhibits mold growth in bread. The effect of this additive in different types of bread as well as the effect of temperature on the preservative will be determined. You will also analyze other methods of preserving food.

Getting Started

Purpose: To determine how effective the food additive calcium propionate is in inhibiting the molding of bread.

Materials

paper towels	marking pen
water	masking tape
6 plastic 1-gallon (4-liter) size zip-lock bags	magnifying lens (handheld type)
6 slices of white bread with propionate	
6 slices of white bread without propionate or any other preservatives	

Procedure

1. Moisten one paper towel with water and lay it inside one plastic bag.

2. Place one slice of bread with propionate and one without side by side on top of the moistened paper towel inside the bag.

3. Zip the plastic bag closed.

4. Use the marking pen and masking tape to label the bread with and without propionate. Place the label on the outside of the bag above the indicated slice of bread.

5. Repeat the procedure (steps 1 through 4) preparing five additional bags with two slices of bread, one slice of bread with propionate and one without, inside each bag. *Note:* Six bags is not a significant number, but it does provide enough samples to verify your results.

6. Keep the six bags of bread at room temperature.

7. Examine the slices each day with the magnifying lens.

8. Continue observing the bread for two weeks or until every slice has become moldy. Record the length of time required for each slice to mold.

Results

Given enough time, all of the bread slices become moldy. However, the slices with calcium propionate mold more slowly. (see Figure 20.1)

Why?

Calcium propionate is a food additive on the U.S. Food and Drug Administration's **GRAS** ("Generally Recognized As Safe") **list**. At low concentrations, it is considered harmless to humans but inhibits the reproduction and growth of mold. The addition of calcium propionate to bread allows the product to be stored for longer periods of time.

Microbes are fussy about their diet, and different species can be found on specific foods. Food preservatives are chemicals added to food to prevent spoilage. Calcium propionate is a preferred preservative for bread because it retards the rapid growth of bread mold, increases the content of calcium, and avoids the possibility of decreasing gas formation during baking.

Try New Approaches

1. How effective is calcium propionate in breads other than white bread? Repeat the experiment using different breads, such as wheat, rye, potato, and raisin. **Science Fair Hint:** Record results of the original as well as this experiment and display the data tables.

2. Does temperature affect the effectiveness of the preservative calcium propionate? Repeat the original experiment using two sets of bread samples. Place one set in the refrigerator and place the second set in a warm area such as on top of a refrigerator. **Science Fair Hint:** Take photographs as each experiment progresses to show the changes in the food as a result of containing or not containing calcium propionate.

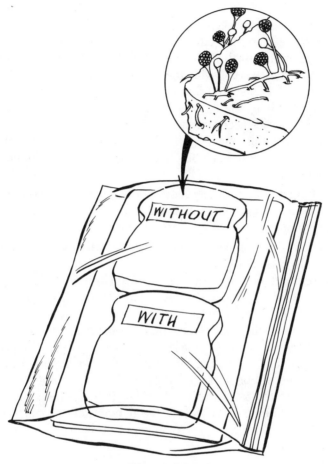

Figure 20.1

Design Your Own Experiment

1. Drying foods was one of the earliest methods of food preservation. This method is based on the fact that the bacteria, mold, and yeast known to spoil food do not grow and reproduce without water. Find out more about procedures for preserving food by drying. Place dried and fresh food samples in open dishes (beef jerky and strips of fresh beef make good samples). Examine the food samples daily for evidence of spoilage and determine the effectiveness of drying as a method of preserving. *Note:* Both samples are inedible and should be discarded after the experiment.

2a. Table salt (sodium chloride) and vinegar (acetic acid) are used as preservatives. Test the effectiveness of these preservatives on inhibiting bacterial growth. Dissolve one chicken bouillon cube in 1 cup (250 ml) of hot water. Divide the solution equally between three clear glasses. Add 1 teaspoon (5 ml) of salt to one glass and 1 teaspoon (5 ml) of vinegar to the second glass. The third glass is the control. Label the glasses accordingly. Place the glasses in a warm place and examine their contents daily. Spoilage due to the presence of bacteria results in a solution that looks cloudy, has an odor, and often contains gas bubbles.

b. Does the amount of preservative added change the results? Repeat the experiment two times, first using less salt and vinegar, and then using a larger quantity of the preservatives.

3. Many foods are spoiled by the growth of various fungi in the food. Favorable conditions such as moisture and temperature encourage rapid reproduction of fungi. Sugar is used as a preservative for fruits because it aids in removing moisture from the cells of the fruit. Fungi are less likely to grow in the dryer fruit. Demonstrate sugar's ability to dehydrate fruit cells by peeling an apple and cutting it into small pieces. Place the pieces into a jar and add ¼ cup (62 ml) of granulated sugar and stir. Secure the lid on the jar. After about 24 hours, the apple pieces will be surrounded by a thick solution of the sugar dissolved in water from the fruit's cells. Use diagrams showing the changes in the jar to represent the dehydrating property of sugar. As part of a display, show examples of products that use sugar as a preservative.

Get the Facts

1. The U.S. Food and Drug Administration (FDA) regulates the use of food additives. Nitrates and nitrites are used as preservatives for meat; they also give meat a healthy-looking red color. These preservatives are potentially dangerous because they can lead to the production of cancer-causing chemicals in the digestive system. FDA regulations allow foods to contain up to 500 parts per million (ppm) of nitrate and 200 ppm of nitrite. It is considered safe for adults to consume these preservatives at this low level, but foods for babies under one year of age should contain no nitrate or nitrite additives. Find out more about

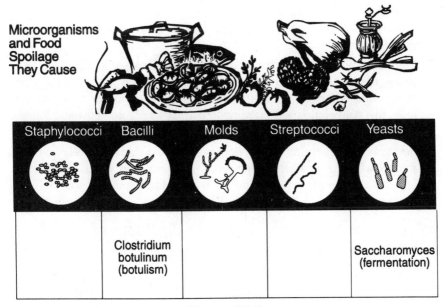

Figure 20.2

nitrates and nitrites. Could other safer methods of preserving meats
be used?

2. The food additive sodium benzoate is on the GRAS list. This chemical
occurs naturally in many foods, such as prunes and cranberries. It is
naturally present and part of the metabolic process in the human body.
Find out more about sodium benzoate. What conditions must exist for
it to be effective? List foods it is used in. What is considered a harmless
level for human consumption?

3. The FDA allows preservatives to be added to foods at specific levels.
How are these safe levels of consumption determined?

4. Five types of microorganisms that cause food to spoil are staphylo-
cocci, bacilli, molds, streptococci, and yeasts. These organisms feed
on much the same substances as do humans and, when present, can
bring about undesirable chemical and physical changes in food. With
the right conditions, they can double in number every 20 or 30 minutes. Find out more about these food spoilers and how they can be
controlled. You could prepare a data table for display showing diagrams of the five types of microorganisms and listing specific types of
food spoilage, such as botulism (one of the most serious types of food

poisoning) or simple fermentation by yeast. (See the sample data table in Figure 20.2.)

5. Find out more about advancements in preserving foods. Compare home food preservation methods in the past and at present. Some things have changed very little, such as the smoking of meats on an open fire. You could use diagrams to compare old and new techniques.

6. In the late-eighteenth century, Napoleon offered 12,000 francs for a new way of preserving food. Nicolas Appert, a Parisian chef, won the money with his heat-preserved foods. Find out how this man without any knowledge of bacteria and its role in food spoilage was able to preserve food.

21 Breathing Rates of Aquatic and Air Breathers

Fish gills remove oxygen from water as human lungs extract oxygen from air. The oxygen content of air is about 20 times as great as richly aerated water. Therefore, aquatic organisms such as fish spend about 20 times more of their energy breathing than do air breathers.

In this project, you will determine the breathing rates of a goldfish and an air breather (human). Factors affecting the breathing rates, such as temperature changes and physical activity, will be studied. *Note:* Treat the goldfish with care at all times. Only take on this project if you or someone you know is willing to keep and maintain the fish after the experiments.

Getting Started

Purpose: To observe the opening of a fish's mouth and its **operculum** (flap of skin covering the gills) to determine the breathing rate of the fish.

Materials

1-quart (1-liter) jar with wide mouth

aquarium water

fishnet

5 or more goldfish of different sizes and body markings

helper

timer

Procedure

Note: The goldfish should be in an aquarium that has been properly prepared according to instructions from a professional at a pet store or from a fish manual. Feeding of the fish should be considered as part of the normal maintenance of the fish and not as an experiment in this project.

1. Prepare a test tank by filling a 1-quart (1-liter) jar half full with water from the aquarium.

Figure 21.1

2. Use the fishnet to carefully transfer the smallest fish from the aquarium to the test jar. Observe the external anatomy of the fish. Record the description and number this fish as 1 in your records so that it can be identified by sight.

3. Wait five minutes to allow the fish to calm after being transferred. Be very quiet and still as you proceed with the experiment.

4. Find the fish's mouth and its operculum (see Figure 21.1).

5. Count the number of times that fish 1 opens and closes its mouth and its operculum over a period of two minutes. Set a timer or ask a helper to assist in timing the experiment.

6. Repeat the counting process (step 5) twice.

7. Average the three trials and divide by 2 to determine the average breathing rate (number of mouth/operculum openings) for one minute. A two-minute observation time is used because small fluctuations are averaged out with longer observation periods.

8. Use the fishnet to carefully return the fish to the aquarium.

Results

The mouth and the operculum open and close an equal number of times. The breathing rate per minute may vary but should be between 100 and 115.

Why?

A fish inhales water; it does not drink water. "Yawning" movements draw water into the mouth, and then the mouth closes. The mouth cavity contracts, forcing the water through the gills and out the operculum, the protective covering over the gills. This rhythmic movement of the mouth and operculum brings in oxygen-rich water to the gills, where the oxygen is extracted. The oxygen-depleted water is then expelled through the operculum.

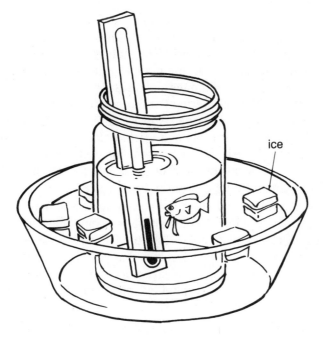

Figure 21.2

Try New Approaches

Does the size of the fish affect its breathing rate? Observe the external anatomy of the other goldfish as they swim in the aquarium. Record descriptions of each fish and number them in order of size (smallest as number 1) in your records so that each can be identified by sight. Repeat the experiment for each of the fish. **Science Fair Hint:** Take photographs of each fish to use as part of your display. Provide information about the breathing rate of each.

Design Your Own Experiment

1. How does temperature affect the breathing rate of fish? Use a fishnet to carefully transfer fish 1 to the test jar. Place a thermometer inside the jar. Set the jar in a bowl half filled with water. Lower the temperature of the water inside the jar by two-to-five degree intervals by adding small pieces of ice to the water in the bowl (see Figure 21.2). Gently stir the water in the jar with each addition of ice to reach a uniform temperature and record that temperature. At each temperature interval, it is important to wait five minutes to allow the fish to adjust to the new temperature. Too sudden a temperature change could injure the fish. Count the number of times the fish opens and closes its mouth in two minutes and divide by 2 for the breathing rate per minute. Continue lowering the temperature until 41° F (5° C) is reached. Do not be concerned if exact temperature increments are reached. Allow the jar to sit and warm before returning the fish to the aquarium. Repeat the experiment for each fish. Construct and display a graph showing the average breathing rate of each fish at each of the different temperatures (see Figure 21.3).

2. Does increased activity affect the breathing rate of fish? Place fish 1 in the test jar. Maintain a constant water temperature. Cover the jar with a dark cloth and do not disturb the fish with noise or movement for five minutes. Position yourself so that you can immediately begin counting mouth movements as you quickly remove the cloth. Determine the startled fish's respiration rate. Repeat the procedure for each fish.

3a. How does the breathing rate of fish compare to that of air breathers such as humans? Choose a test subject. Count the number of times the person breathes during two minutes. Repeat the counting process twice. Average the three trials and divide by 2 to calculate the breathing rate of the person for one minute. Make an effort not to inform the person that you are observing his or her breathing.

b. Does the breathing rate change if the person is aware of being observed? Repeat the experiment explaining to the test subject what you are doing.

c. How does exercise affect the breathing rate of air breathers? Repeat the experiment twice, first measuring the breathing rate of the test subject at rest, and then measuring the rate after the subject has quickly marched in place for two minutes. Be sure that this exercise does not endanger the health of the test subject.

d. Use a photograph of your human test subject and a photograph of one of the test fish to represent the breathing rates of air and water breathers. Display information about the breathing rates and diagrams of air breathers that are more comparable in size to the fish.

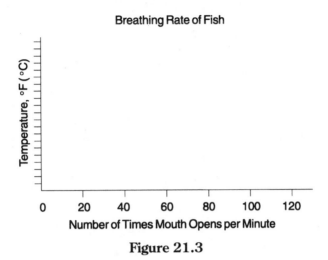

Figure 21.3

Get the Facts

1. The breathing of a fish is like a two-way pump. Water is pulled into the mouth and pushed out the gills. Use a biology text or science encyclopedia to find out more about this mechanical process and how oxygen is extracted from the water. What is the purpose of gill filaments and gill rakers?

2. The requirement of oxygen for a fish changes with water temperature. As the temperature rises, the metabolism of the fish increases; thus, more oxygen is needed. At the same time, at a higher temperature water cannot hold as much dissolved oxygen; thus, the fish has to inhale more water to meet its oxygen demand. Use a biology text to find published values for oxygen content of water at different temperatures and the oxygen-consumption requirement of fish per weight unit. Use a pharmacy scale to determine the exact weight of your fish. Place one fish in a jar of water and weigh it. Weigh the jar with the exact amount of water without the fish. Calculate the weight of the fish. Do this for each fish and use the weights to determine the ventilation rate (amount of water inhaled per weight unit per hour) of each fish.

22 Drosophila Metamorphosis

Fruit flies (*Drosophila melanogaster*) are often used as research specimens because they are small, easily obtained, and easy to maintain. Their fast reproductive cycle makes them favorable specimens for studying the process of metamorphosis.

In this project, you will observe the general life cycle of the fruit fly. Each stage of the metamorphosis will be timed, and effects of temperature on these times will be determined. You will examine the desired environment for development as well as the percentage of males and females produced in each generation.

Flies can carry diseases. When the experiments are completed, put the jar of flies in a freezer for at least one hour. Dead flies have their wings sticking out to the sides. Discard the dead flies.

Getting Started

Purpose: To observe the life cycle of fruit flies (*Drosophila melanogaster*).

Materials

overripe banana
1-quart (1-liter) jar
paper towel
rubber band
magnifying lens

Procedure

1. Peel the banana and place it into the open jar.
2. Set the jar outside.
3. Observe the jar. After several flies are seen in the jar, wait 30 minutes and wave the jar back and forth to swish the flies out.
4. Bring the jar inside.
5. Cover the mouth of the jar with the paper towel and secure the paper with the rubber band.
6. Allow the jar to stand undisturbed for 14 days.

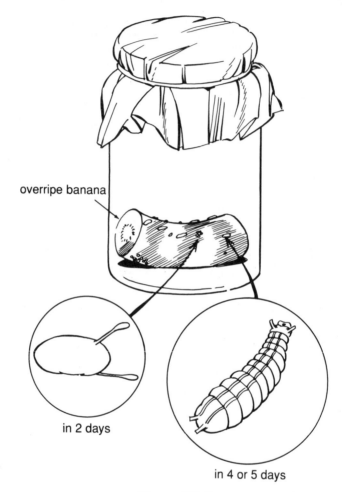

overripe banana

in 2 days

in 4 or 5 days

Figure 22.1

7. Use the magnifying lens to observe the contents of the jar. Make note of all changes.

8. Keep the flies in the jar for further experimentation.

Results

Small, white, moist-looking specks on the surface of the banana change into white wormlike creatures within two days (see Figure 22.1). At the end of four or five days, objects the color and shape of wheat grain can be seen stuck to the inside wall of the jar at various heights. Flies appear in the jar in another ten days.

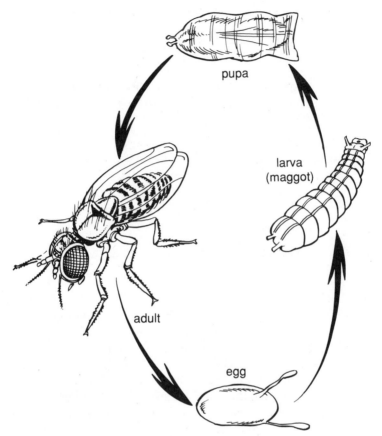

Figure 22.2   Fly Metamorphosis

Why?

The **metamorphosis** (development of an insect by passing through several stages) of the fly involves four separate stages (see Figure 22.2). In the first stage, there is the **egg,** which is elliptical and has two small projections on one end. These projections enable it to float in liquid mediums. In the second stage, which occurs within 24 to 48 hours after the first, the egg develops into a **larva.** The larva is the white wormlike organism commonly called a *maggot.* By eating continually, the larva forms channels in the fruit. After about four days, the larva crawls onto the side of the jar, contracts, and becomes more elliptical in shape. At this point, it enters the third, or **pupa,** stage. The larva is still white; however, within hours it darkens. No motion is observed during the pupa stage, but it is

Rate of Metamorphosis	
Day	Observations
1	Eggs are seen on the surface of the fruit. Eggs are elliptical in shape and have two projections on one end. 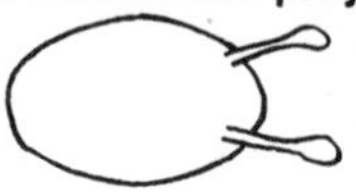
2	
3	

Figure 22.3

during this period that legs, wings, and a head develop. About ten days later, the fourth and final stage is reached and a pale-colored, fragile fly emerges. Shortly thereafter, the fly darkens in color.

Male and female flies can be identified. Male flies are noticeably smaller and have a pointed posterior that ends in a sort of "button." The rear end of the male's abdomen has intense black coloring that extends around the sides to meet **ventrally** (in the front, near the bottom). Females have small, black-colored lines across the abdomen that are confined to the upper part and never meet underneath. *Note:* Sexes are difficult to distinguish by color until the flies are a few hours old because newly emerged flies are very pale.

Try New Approaches

1. Determine for yourself the times required for each stage of a fly's metamorphosis. Repeat the experiment. Make daily observations starting with the appearance of eggs and noting the time required for the appearance of each new stage of development. **Science Fair Hint:** Record your data in a table, starting with day 1 and including a sketch and a description of each stage of development. Use the data table as part of your project display (see the sample data table in Figure 22.3).

2. Does temperature affect the length of time needed for complete metamorphosis? Repeat the original experiment preparing three different jars. Place one jar at room temperature, the second in a warm area (such as near a water heater), and, for sanitary reasons, the third inside a box that can be closed and placed in a refrigerator. Keep a daily record of development in each environment and of the temperature of each.

Design Your Own Experiment

1. Young feeding larvae are physically adapted to live in moist conditions. Older mature larvae like a dryer environment. Demonstrate this by filling a small vial, such as a medicine bottle, about three-fourths full with pieces of banana. Set the vial inside a 1-quart (1-liter) jar. Place a male and a female fly into the vial. Cover the mouth of the jar with a paper towel and secure the paper with a rubber band. Observe the contents of the jar daily until the flies reproduce and the larvae enter the pupa stage (about seven days).

2. What percentage of each fly generation is female? What percentage is male? Wrap a strip of paper towel around a 2-inch (5-cm) slice of banana. Place the banana into a 1-pint (500-ml) jar. Place a male and a female fly into the jar. The metamorphosis of the fly is complete in about two weeks. Wait another two days to allow the flies to mature and then place the jar in a freezer for one hour to kill the flies. Remove the jar and shake the flies out of the jar and onto a sheet of paper. Use a magnifying lens to observe the flies and count the number of each sex. Repeat two times. Find the average percentages.

3. What changes occur during the pupa stage? Examine the pupa when it is complete. Break open one puparium (outer shell) each day and record the contents. Do this until the flies start to emerge. At the beginning of the pupa stage, the larva contracts and its outer tissue darkens. This darkening is from sclerotization of the larval cuticle. What is sclerotization?

Get the Facts

1. The common housefly has six legs just as other insects do. Its feet have claws and sticky hairs that aid in locomotion. The tips of the hairs must be free of dust to allow the fly to stick well and thus walk on smooth surfaces easily. The fly can be seen cleaning its feet constantly by rubbing them against each other and its body. Find out more about the physical structure of the housefly and other flies. Do they bite? How are they alike and how do they differ from other insects?

2. The metamorphosis of the housefly is complete in about two weeks. Flies multiply rapidly and produce about 200 or more eggs at a time. What if the reproduction was unchecked and all the offspring survived? Prepare a data table similar to the one shown here to indicate the reproduction of flies during four generations, starting with the eggs from only one female. Assume that half of the eggs are females in each generation and that each female lays 200 eggs.

Unchecked Fly Population Data Table			
Week	Generation	Calculation	Number of Flies
0	1	——	200
2	2	100 × 200 =	20,000
4	3	10,000 × 200 =	2,000,000
6	4		

3. Fruit flies (*Drosophila melanogaster*) have large chromosomes in the salivary glands of the larvae. From these more visible chromosomes, what have researchers discovered about the genetic traits of flies? How do the chromosomes of male and female flies differ? What has been discovered about the sex chromosomes of the flies and how does this affect the number of females and males produced in each generation?

4. A fruit fly egg contains one X sex chromosome, and the sperm has either an X or a Y sex chromosome. A Punnett square is a special grid used to show the possible combinations of genes. Find out more about the Punnett square and use it to depict the results of random union of a sperm and an egg.

23 Interactions in an Open Ecosystem

In nature, there is a constant interaction among animals, plants, fungi, protists—microorganisms not easily classified as fungi, plant or animal—and their environment. In this ecosystem, there is a direct relationship between the community of living organisms and its surroundings. The organisms affect their physical surroundings just as they are affected by them.

In this project, you will observe some of these interactions in an open ecosystem and investigate populations within a sector. You will also determine populations of organisms by using the technique of random sampling.

Getting Started

Purpose: To select and lay out a study area.

Materials

compass

measuring tape

hammer

12 wooden or metal tent stakes

300 yards (300 m) of cord

graph paper

Procedure

1. Select a study area that has a variation of plant life. (A wooded area was chosen by the author, but any ecosystem can be used.)

2. Use the compass to determine which direction is north.

3. With the measuring tape, measure an area 30 × 30 yards (30 × 30 m). The plot of ground should be measured so that it is aligned in a north-to-south direction.

4. At each of the four corners of the plot, hammer one stake into the ground, leaving about 6 inches (15 cm) of the stake aboveground.

5. Attach the end of the cord to one stake, loop it around the other stakes, and tie it to the starting stake to enclose the plot.

6. Use the measuring tape to divide the sides of the plot into 10-yard (10-m) sections.

7. Drive one stake into the ground at each 10-yard (10-m) interval along all sides of the plot (see Figure 23.1).

8. Using cord to join opposite stakes, divide the plot into nine equal subplots.

9. On graph paper, sketch the plot. Identify each subplot with a number. Indicate the compass directions with arrows on the sketch.

10. Make separate sketches of each subplot. Note prominent land features such as trails, open areas, erosion, and streams.

Results

A sampling plot of ground is selected, measured, and subdivided. A general description of prominent land features is noted.

Why?

The sampling plot allows you to sample and study **biotic factors** (relationships among organisms) and **abiotic factors** (the physical aspects of an environment; temperature, erosion, the slope of the land). In this field study, measurements of physical factors and organisms can be taken. Separate information taken from each subplot, when studied as a whole, provides a clear picture of the **ecological community** (interaction of living organisms with their environment) within the plot and gives clues to the surrounding **ecosystem** (ecological community).

Try New Approaches

1. Construct and use an Abney level to measure the angle of the slope of the land of each subplot. Make the level by using masking tape to attach a protractor to the center of a yardstick (meterstick). Tie a 12-inch (30-cm) piece of string to the center of the protractor and attach a washer to the free end of the string (see Figure 23.2). Hold the measuring stick parallel to the ground of each subplot while a helper reads the angle on the protractor made by the hanging string. When the slope is zero, the string hangs straight down across the 90° mark. To determine the angle of slopes, subtract the angle reading from 90°. For example, if the protractor reads 50°, the angle of the slope is 90° − 50°, or 40°.

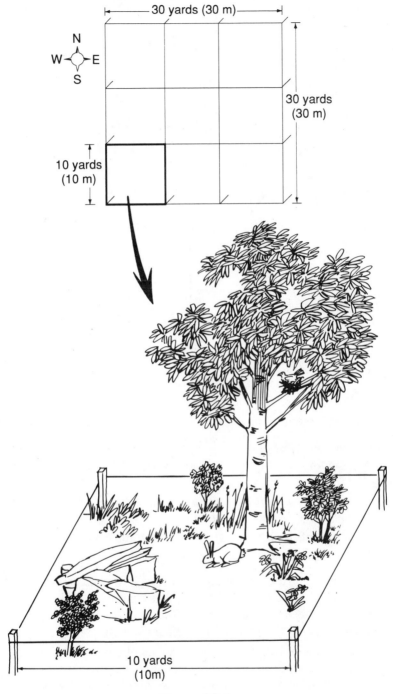

Figure 23.1

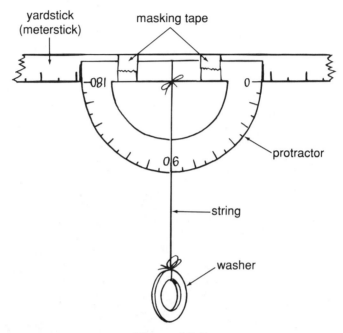

Figure 23.2

2. Observe the types of plants in each subplot. The four types of plants that you may find and their typical description within each subplot are as follows:

   ▪ herbaceous (nonwoody) plants—vegetation such as fern, grass, weeds, moss, lichen, and fungi.

   ▪ woody plants—shrubs with two or more main stems.

   ▪ trees—woody plants with one main stem.

   Count and record the number of each type of plant found within the sampling area of each subplot. Use these numbers and sample problems from Appendix 3 to determine the abundance and frequency percentages as well as the density for each plant type.

3. Record the actual presence or indications of the presence of animals. Note the presence of tracks, holes, sounds, claw marks, hair, nests, and so on. Cautiously turn over rocks and logs to discover insects, reptiles, and amphibians. Remember that you are an observer and do not want to change this ecosystem, so return rocks and logs to their original positions.

4. Make an insect net by bending a coat hanger into a hoop. Attach small-holed netting sewn in the shape and size of a pillowcase to the hoop (or a pillowcase can be used instead). Secure the ends of the hoop to a broom handle. Walk across each subplot in a straight line. Sweep the net back and forth as you walk across each plot. Close the net. Empty the contents of the net into a jar and secure the lid. Label the jar with the plot number. Collect insects in each plot. Record the number and type of insects found in each plot. **Science Fair Hint:** Display the collected insects in small baby food jars containing rubbing alcohol. Place identification labels on each jar.

5. Determine the number and identity of arthropods (joint-legged animals) in leaf litter found on the ground in each subplot. Use your hands to remove the leaf litter from a 10-×-10-inch (25-×-25-cm) sampling area. Pour the leaf litter into a funnel (some will fall through, but most will pack and stay in the open funnel). Push a paper towel around the top surface of the litter to prevent organisms from crawling out. Stand the funnel in a jar with about 2 inches (5 cm) of alcohol in it. Place a desk lamp above the funnel. As the leaf litter heats and dries, the organisms will crawl to the bottom and fall into the alcohol. This may take several days, so add alcohol as it evaporates.

CAUTION: Alcohol is flammable. Do not use it near an open flame. Wash your hands after using alcohol.

6. Beneath the leaf litter in each subplot, collect a baby-food-size jar full of soil. Analyze soil samples for organisms by lining a food colander with fine-mesh screen. Support the colander with a bucket. Spread the soil sample over the mesh screen. Slowly pour water over the soil until the soil washes away. Turn the screen over on a paper towel and use tweezers or forceps to sort through the material. Use a dissecting microscope, if available, to observe and identify macrofauna (larger than 1 cm), mesofauna (0.2 to 1 cm), and microfauna (less than 0.2 cm) present.

Design Your Own Experiment

1. Collect leaf samples from the plants and, using plant field guides, identify the types of each plant present. You could display photographs of the plants along with preserved samples of the leaves or leaf rubbings.

See Appendix 4 for techniques for preserving plants and making rubbings.

2. Make molds of tracks by pouring plaster of paris into the tracks. Mix
this liquid by following the directions on the box of plaster of paris.
You could use the molds as part of a project display.

Get the Facts

1. When an organism feeds upon another living thing, there is a transfer
of materials and energy. This transfer from organism to organism is
called a *food chain*. Find out more about the food chain. What is a food
web? What is a pyramid of energy and a pyramid of numbers? Use the
information collected in your plot to construct a pyramid of numbers.

2. Energy is constantly lost in an ecosystem and has to be replaced by
sunlight. There is also a fixed amount of matter within the system.
Find out how matter is recycled in an ecosystem.

PART III

The Human Body

Functions of the Human Breathing Mechanism

24

You do not make a conscious decision for your lungs to take in and expel air. A part of the brain called the medulla oblongata controls your respiratory system. Impulses are sent to the medulla as signals from your body that the oxygen supply in the cells is too low and the carbon dioxide content is too high. These messages trigger the respiratory system to increase the breathing rate and depth of breathing. Thus, excess carbon dioxide is released and oxygen is taken in by the body. This regulating mechanism keeps the carbon dioxide and oxygen levels within limits tolerable for life.

In this project, you will have the opportunity to study the lung capacity and measurement of tidal air (air in normal breathing), reserve air (air forced out after a normal expiration), and complemental air (forced amount of air that can be inhaled). Factors affecting the lung capacity, such as gender and athletic ability, will also be studied. Functions of various parts of the breathing mechanism will be determined via a lung model, and you will examine the effect of factors such as age, gender, and exercise on the breathing rate.

Getting Started

Purpose: To measure lung air capacity.

Materials

masking tape

1-gallon (4-liter) glass jug with lid

1-cup (250-ml) measuring cup

water

marking pen

large plastic dishpan

helper

2-foot (60-cm) piece of aquarium tubing

drinking straw

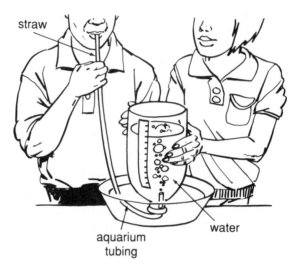

straw

aquarium
tubing

water

Figure 24.1

Procedure

1. Place a strip of masking tape down the side of the glass jug.

2. Use the measuring cup to add 16 cups (4 liters) of water to the jug, 1 cup (250 ml) at a time. Use the marking pen to mark a line on the tape to indicate the height after each cup of water.

3. Secure the lid on the jug.

4. Fill the dishpan about half full with water.

5. Place the jug upside down in the dishpan and remove the lid.

6. Ask your helper to hold the jug. Do not allow air bubbles to enter the jug.

7. Place about 4 inches (10 cm) of one end of the tubing into the mouth of the jug.

8. Insert the drinking straw into the free end of the tubing to make a sanitary mouthpiece (see Figure 24.1).

9. Take a normal breath and exhale through the straw into the tubing.

10. Use the scale on the jug to determine the amount of your exhaled breath. Record this measurement as tidal air.

11. Refill the jar with water. Inhale normally and exhale through the straw into the tubing, making an effort to force all of the air from your lungs. Record this measurement as tidal air + reserve air.

12. Refill the jug. Inhale deeply and force out all of the air you can from your lungs. Record this measurement as **vital capacity** (maximum volume of air inhaled or exhaled during forced breathing). Vital capacity is the tidal air + reserve air + complemental air.

13. Use your measurements to calculate reserve and complemental air, then fill in a data table such as the one shown here.

Results

Data Table Chart for Author	
Lung Capacity	Measurement
tidal air reserve air complemental air	27 cubic inches (0.45 liter) 85 cubic inches (1.42 liters) 110 cubic inches (1.83 liters)
Total vital capacity	222 cubic inches (3.70 liters)

Why?

When the lungs are filled, they hold varying amounts of air depending on the size of the person. The author's lungs hold about 222 cubic inches (3.70 liters). About 27 cubic inches (0.45 liter) of this amount is tidal air. **Tidal air** is the amount of air involved during normal, relaxed **inspiration** (breathing in) and **expiration** (breathing out). The amount of air that can be forced out after normal expiration is called **reserve air,** and the amount of air that can be inhaled with force is called **complemental air.** With vigorous inspiration and expiration, the tidal air + reserve air + complemental air (or total vital capacity) can be expelled. Even with maximum expiration, the lungs are not empty. There is always about 60 cubic inches (1 liter) of air left in the lungs, and this amount is referred to as **residual air.**

Try New Approaches

Do gender and athletic ability affect the vital capacity of the lungs? Repeat the experiment testing groups of people of different genders and athletic abilities.

Design Your Own Experiment

1. Inspiration and expiration result from changes in the chest cavity. Build a lung model to demonstrate the effect of pressure changes within a closed area and relate this to the pressure changes within the chest cavity. Cut out the bottom of a 2-liter plastic soda bottle. Push the tip of the balloon inside the bottle and pull the mouth of the balloon over the mouth of the bottle. Cover the opening at the bottom of the bottle with a piece of plastic cut from a garbage bag. Secure the plastic with a rubber band. Roll a 4-inch (10-cm) piece of duct tape, sticky side out, into a circle, and attach it to the center of the plastic (see Figure 24.2). Hold the bottle and use your fingers to move the surface of the plastic in and out by pulling and pushing on the tape. Observe the size of the balloon as the plastic moves. Compare the parts of the model to the lung, chest cavity, and diaphragm of the human body. Use the model and diagrams as part of a project display.

2a. Determine the breathing rate for a person at rest. Choose a test subject. Count the number of times the person breathes during two minutes. Repeat the counting process twice. Average the three trials and divide by 2 to calculate the breathing rate of the person for one minute. Make an effort not to inform the person that you are observing his or her breathing to prevent any change in normal breathing.

b. Determine whether factors such as age, exercise, or gender affect breathing rate. Select test subjects of different ages and an equal number of each gender. Repeat the experiment to determine the normal resting breathing rate for each test subject. Then determine the effect of exercise on the breathing rate of each person in the test group by having each one perform a timed exercise (such as marching in place for two minutes). Choose an exercise that each person in the group can perform without endangering his or her health.

3. The rate and depth of inspiration are much greater after a period of breath-holding because of the buildup of carbon dioxide inside the lungs. Demonstrate this by determining the breathing rate and the expansion of the chest of a test subject during normal rest breathing. Have the subject hold his or her breath as long as possible without becoming dizzy. Observe the expansion of the chest and determine the breathing rate after the breath-holding period.

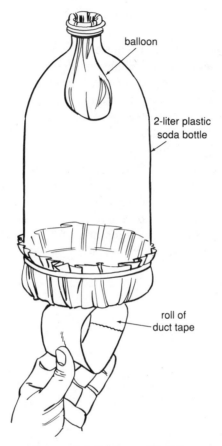

balloon

2-liter plastic
soda bottle

roll of
duct tape

Figure 24.2   Lung Model

4. A simple cure for **hyperventilation** (extravigorous breathing) is to breathe into a paper bag for several minutes. How does breathing into the bag affect breathing rate and volume of air taken in? Determine the breathing rate and the expansion of the chest of a test subject during normal rest breathing. Then have the test subject breathe into and out of a paper bag for one minute. Immediately after, determine the person's breathing rate and observe the expansion of his or her chest. **CAUTION:** Do not use a platic bag.

Get the Facts

1. Breathing, a purely mechanical process, involves bringing air with oxygen into the body and expelling air rich in carbon dioxide out of the body. The lungs are spongy, air-filled sacs that contain no muscles and cannot expand or contract on their own. By what mechanism is air moved into and out of the lungs? Use a biology text to find out more about this mechanical process. Through what passageways is the air transported into and out of the body?

2. Victims of drowning accidents, electrocution, or heart attacks need oxygen for survival. Because normal breathing does not supply enough oxygen, resuscitators are used. Resuscitators are tanks of compressed oxygen that force oxygen into a victim's lungs. Find out more about this life-saving equipment. Why is carbon dioxide added to a resuscitator's tank of oxygen? How much is added?

25 Effectiveness of Sunscreens

Exposure of skin to rays from the sun is unavoidable, but many people purposely bathe their bodies in these rays to achieve a "perfect tan." Some people want to prevent overexposure and pain of sunburn. Many manufacturers provide suntan products that are advertised to protect the skin from the sun and promote tanning.

In this project, you will determine the screening ability of suntan lotions and determine whether sunblock lotions are more effective than tanning lotions. You will also examine the relationship between cost and effectiveness of sunscreening products.

Getting Started

Purpose: To test the effectiveness of suntan lotions.

Materials

masking tape

clear plastic report folder

marking pen

4 brands of sunblock lotion with
   the same SPF

Sunprint photographic paper
   (Purchase this paper at a
   nature or toy store.)

tap water

Procedure

1. Use masking tape to divide the top sheet of the report folder into four equal parts. Position the pieces of tape so that one goes down and one goes across the center of the folder.

2. With the marking pen, number each of the four sections.

3. Assign a number to each brand of lotion and record it in a data table.

4. Use your fingers to coat each section of the plastic with the corresponding brand of lotion. Wash your hands before applying each brand and make sure you apply equal thicknesses of lotion to each section.

5. In a semidarkened room, remove a sheet of developing paper from its protective container. Close the container tightly to protect the remaining sheets from light exposure.

6. Raise the lotion-coated plastic and place the sheet of developing paper, glossy side up, inside the folder.

7. Close the folder and set it, lotion side up, outside in the sun (see A in Figure 25.1). Best results occur at midday when the sun's rays are most direct.

8. After five minutes, return the folder to the darkened room.

9. Follow the instructions on package to fix the photographic paper.

10. Allow the paper to dry.

11. Observe the degree of coloration on each section of the paper (see B in figure 25.1). Record your results in a data table such as the one shown here.

12. Repeat the procedure twice.

Sunblock Lotion Data Table				
		Results		
Brand	Number	Trial 1	Trial 2	Trial 3
	1			
	2			
	3			
	4			

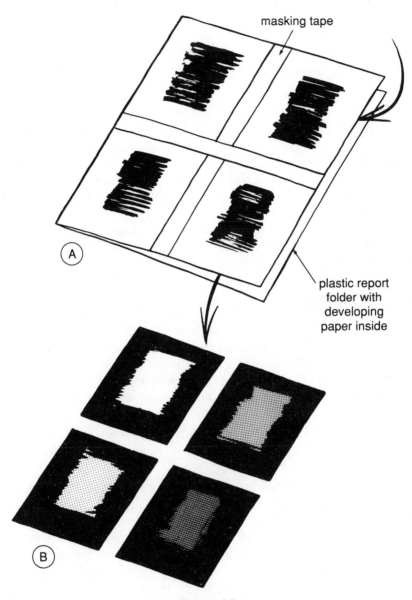

Figure 25.1

Results

The Sunprint paper remains unchanged under the strips of tape. Under the lotions, the paper has degrees of darkness.

Why?

Sunprint photographic paper is coated with a light-sensitive compound. Exposure to light, like the sun, chemically changes the compound producing a dark color. The amount of change depends on the amount of light that falls on the paper. Thus, the areas shielded from light by the tape remain white. The degree of darkness in the area shielded by the lotions in this experiment indicates the effectiveness of each lotion in blocking out the sun's rays. The water removes the light-sensitive compound on the paper; thus, the image on the paper is fixed (made permanent) so that light no longer turns it dark and you have a permanent record of your results.

Try New Approaches

1. Do suntan lotions give as much protection as sunblock lotions? Repeat the experiment using samples of suntan and sunblock lotions. **Science Fair Hint:** Use the exposed Sunprint paper from the different experiments as part of a project display. Label each to indicate the lotion used. Take photographs during the experiment to represent the procedure.

2. Is there a difference in the protection of differently rated sunblock lotions? Repeat the original experiment using sunblock lotions with low to high number ratings.

3. Does the price of the product affect how it works? Repeat the original experiment using sunblocks with the same rating but different prices. Do more expensive lotions offer more protection? Divide the product prices into three groups and let each group represent a price range. **Science Fair Hint:** Use a bar graph to represent your results (see the sample in Figure 25.2).

Design Your Own Experiment

1. If sunlight causes tanning, does an absence of sunlight cause the skin to lighten? Place an adhesive bandage around the end of one finger. Leave the bandage on for 2 days. Remove the bandage and observe the color of the skin over the entire finger.

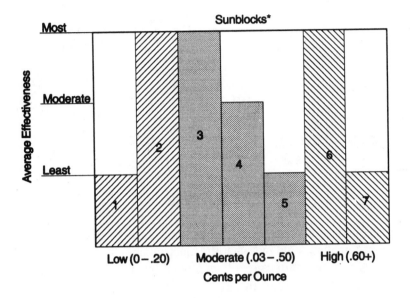

Figure 25.2

2. Does the absence of sunlight affect all skin colors in the same manner? Test a group of people of different skin colors ranging from pale to dark brown. Ask each person to place an adhesive bandage around the end of one finger. After two days, remove the bandages and observe the color of the skin over the entire finger of each person tested.

Get the Facts

1. Sun lotions and creams protect by absorbing radiation. Most sun-protecting products absorb radiation in the critical range of 2,900 to

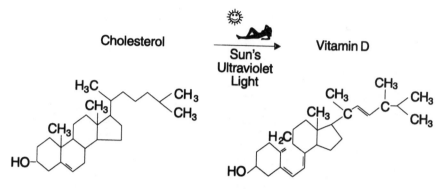

Figure 25.3

3,200 angstroms. Use chemistry and physics texts to gain information about radiation. Find out what the electromagnetic spectrum is. What part of the spectrum causes tanning and burning of the skin?

2. Lotions help to screen the skin from harmful solar rays. A greater protector is the earth's atmosphere. Find out how this envelope of gas around the earth shields the planet from the sun's powerful radiation. What changes in the atmosphere have resulted from pollution? What, if any, effect have the atmospheric changes had on increased skin disorders?

3. The skin color of animals is affected by special cells called *melanocytes.* These cells contain a black pigment called *melanin* that is responsible for skin color, freckles, and suntans. Find out how light affects melanin. What effect does light have on the skin color changes in animals such as chameleons?

4. The sun's rays are not all bad. When the skin is exposed to sunlight, cholesterol, a fat-related compound that is an essential part of many body cells, is converted to vitamin D. Find out about the uses of vitamin D. You could display the uses of vitamin D with a structural diagram showing the change of cholesterol to vitamin D in the presence of ultraviolet light (see Figure 25.3).

26 Function of Digestive Enzymes

In an adult human, food makes about a 30-foot (9-m) trip through the body as it is systematically broken down in preparation for use by body tissues. The pathway begins in the mouth, runs through the esophagus, stomach, and small intestine, and ends in the large intestine.

In this project, you will test for the presence of glucose and starch and determine the function of digestive enzymes in breaking down starch. You will use models to demonstrate the movement of molecules through a semipermeable membrane and the movement of foods through the digestive tract via peristalsis. The absorbency of the intestine due to its structure will also be simulated.

Getting Started

Purpose: To determine a positive test for starch and glucose.

Materials

tablespoon (15 ml)

1% starch solution (see Appendix 2)

3 small baby-food jars (or test tubes)

marking pen

masking tape

Tes-Tape® (glucose enzymatic test strips found at a pharmacy)

eyedropper

tincture of iodine

½ cup (125 ml) of apple juice without added sugar

distilled water

Procedure

CAUTION: Keep the iodine out of reach of small children. It is poisonous and is for external use only.

1. Pour 2 tablespoons (30 ml) of the starch solution into one small jar. With the marking pen, write "Starch" on a piece of masking tape and tape this label to the jar.

2. Test for the presence of glucose in the starch solution by dipping the end of a 1-inch (2.5-cm) strip of Tes-Tape into the solution. Remove the strip and wait two minutes. Compare the color of the strip to the color chart on the Tes-Tape container.

3. Record the color of the Tes-Tape and use the color chart to determine the percentage of glucose in the solution (see Figure 26.1).

4. Test for the presence of starch by adding three drops of iodine to the starch solution, swirl to mix, and record the resulting color.

5. Pour 2 tablespoons (30 ml) of the apple juice into the second small jar. (Apple juice contains glucose and will be used as a positive test for glucose.) Label the jar, "Glucose."

6. Dip a strip of Tes-Tape into the apple juice. After two minutes, record its color and percentage of glucose.

7. Add three drops of iodine to the apple juice, swirl, and record the resulting color.

8. Pour two tablespoons (30 ml) of distilled water into the third jar. Label the jar, "Control."

9. Dip a strip of Tes-Tape into the water and record its color and percentage of glucose.

10. Add three drops of iodine to the water, swirl, and record the resulting color.

Results

Iodine turns the starch solution blue-black; in the apple juice and water, the color is amber. The Tes-Tape remains yellow after being dipped into the water and starch solution; in the apple juice, the tape turns a dark green.

Why?

A positive test for the presence of starch is a blue to blue-black color when iodine is added to the solution. The color is due to the presence of the iodine–starch compound. A positive test for the presence of glucose using the Tes-Tape is a green color. The darker the green, the greater the percentage of glucose in the solution. The control is used to show that water does not change the color of iodine or Tes-Tape.

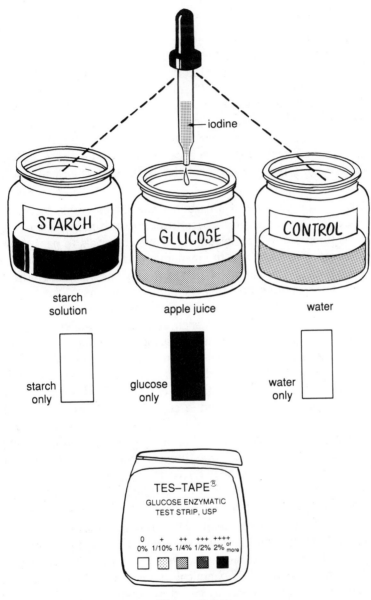

Figure 26.1

Try New Approaches

1a. Are starch and glucose molecules the same size? To determine whether there is a difference in the size of starch and glucose molecules, mix together ½ cup (125 ml) of water, ½ cup (125 ml) of 1% starch solution, and ½ cup (125 ml) of apple juice (contains glucose). Line a funnel with five thicknesses of coffee filters. Pour the mixture of water, starch, and apple juice into the paper-lined funnel. Use the procedure in the experiment to test the filtrate (liquid that passes through the filter) for the presence of starch and glucose. Molecules that are too large to pass through the thick layer of paper will not appear in the filtrate.

b. Starch is an example of a carbohydrate. In its edible form, starch molecules are too large to pass through the semipermeable membrane (membrane that selectively allows materials to pass through) of the digestive tract and too insoluble to dissolve in the blood. Glucose is a much smaller molecule and readily passes through the small holes in the membrane lining the digestive organs.

Demonstrate the selectivity of a semipermeable membrane and the ability or lack of ability of starch and glucose molecules to move through the membrane. Sausage casing (the lining of an intestine) behaves as a semipermeable membrane. Use a 1-foot (30 cm) piece of sausage casing (purchased from a meat market). Tie a knot in one end of the casing. Mix together ¼ cup (63 ml) of water, ¼ cup (63 ml) of 1% starch solution, and ¼ cup (63 ml) of apple juice without added sugar. Pour the mixture into the sausage casing and tie the open end tightly. Place the casing in a jar and add enough water to cover it (see Figure 26.2). Use the procedure in the original experiment to test the liquid outside the casing for glucose. Test for glucose every ten minutes for one hour. At the end of the hour, test the liquid with iodine for the presence of starch.

2. The digestion of large, insoluble starch molecules begins in the mouth. First, the food is physically ground by the teeth and then is chemically broken into smaller molecules. Saliva contains an enzyme called **amylase.** It is this chemical that breaks starch into a smaller **disaccharide** (double sugar) called **maltose.**

Study the effects of saliva on a starch by testing for the presence of glucose and starch in an unchewed and a chewed cracker. *Note:* Use *only* your own saliva to do this experiment. Or, check with your teacher about replacing the saliva with a .1% diatase solution. Wash your hands and then place a clean bite-size piece of a saltine cracker

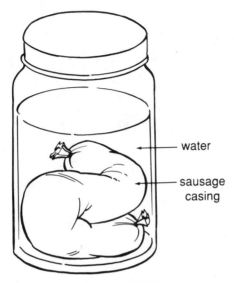

water

sausage
casing

Figure 26.2

into your mouth. Chew and move the cracker around until it is a liquid mush (the longer you chew, the better the results). Place the chewed cracker into a jar and label it "Chewed." Label a second jar "Unchewed" and place an equal-size piece of cracker into it. Add 1 tablespoon (15 ml) of water and mix to form a mush. Repeat the original experiment to test for starch and glucose in the two samples. *Note:* Disinfect containers containing saliva by washing them with a 5:1 bleach solution (5 parts water and 1 part bleach). **CAUTION:** Take care not to get bleach on skin or clothes. It can damage skin and decolorize clothing.

Design Your Own Experiment

1. Food is transported from the mouth to the stomach and on through the digestive tract by a motion known as **peristalsis.** The smooth muscles in the walls of the digestive organs squeeze and contract in a wavelike motion that pushes the food ahead of the contracted area. Demonstrate peristalsis motion in the esophagus by moving a marble through a rubber tube in which the marble fits tightly. Push on the tube behind the marble (see Figure 26.3). Use a diagram to compare the movement of the marble through the rubber tube to movement of a **bolus** (wet ball of partially digested food) through the esophagus.

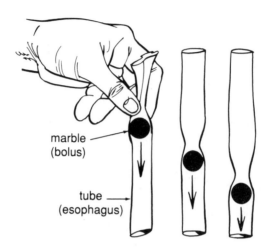

marble
(bolus)

tube
(esophagus)

Figure 26.3

2. Does the shape of an intestine increase absorbency? Folded paper towels take up less space but can absorb more liquid as do the folds in the
lining of the intestine. Demonstrate this by folding one paper towel in
half four times to form a small square. Prepare a measuring jar by
placing a piece of masking tape down the side of the jar. Fill the jar
with water and mark the water level. Dip the folded paper square into
the jar of water. Remove the paper and mark the new water level. Refill
the jar to the first water level and dip a paper square made with three
folded paper towels. Compare the difference in the water removed by
the two squares. More information about this can be found in the experiment titled "Folds" (p. 98) in Janice VanCleave's *Biology for Every
Kid.* (New York: Wiley, 1990).

Get the Facts

Learn more about the digestive system. Use a biology text to examine
the structure and function of each organ in the system. Find out about
the chemical changes that occur and the chemicals involved in promoting
the changes (such as amylase, gastric juices, and bile). What is the difference between a bolus and a chyme? Where are most of the nutrients from
the food absorbed into the bloodstream and lymph system? How long
does it take for the stomach to empty after a meal?

27 Food Changes in the Digestive Tract

Food placed in the mouth is too large and not water soluble enough to be used by the body. Teeth are used to tear apart a large piece of food and grind it into small pieces. The teeth just begin the process of shaping food so that it can be digested. Chemicals in the human digestive system continue to reshape the food at a molecular level as they break apart large food molecules into more usable smaller molecules.

In this project you will test the effectiveness of artificial food enzymes in breaking down starch. Tests will be made to determine any differences in the effectiveness of various manufacturers' processed food enzymes. You will also study factors affecting the function of digestive enzymes, such as concentration of the enzyme and substrate and acidic and alkaline pH.

Getting Started

Purpose: To determine the effect of an enzyme on starch.

Materials

tablespoon (15 ml)

1% starch solution (see Appendix 2)

2 small baby food jars (or test tubes)

marking pen

masking tape

4 eyedroppers

food enzyme (found at a pharmacy)

Tes-Tape® (glucose enzymatic test strips found at a pharmacy)

wax paper

tincture of iodine

12 toothpicks

Procedure

1. Pour 1 tablespoon (15 ml) of the starch solution into each of the two small jars.

2. With the marking pen, write "Control" on a piece of masking tape and tape this label to one jar.

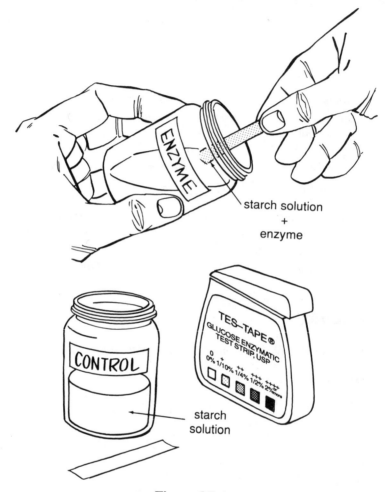

starch solution
+
enzyme

CONTROL

starch
solution

Figure 27.1

3. Label the second jar "Enzyme" and add ten drops of food enzyme.

4. Test for the presence of glucose in each of the jars by dipping the end of a 1-inch (2.5-cm) strip of Tes-Tape into each solution (see Figure 27.1). Remove the strip and wait two minutes. Compare the color of the strip to the color chart on the Tes-Tape container.

5. Record the color of the Tes-Tape and use the color chart to determine the percentage of glucose in each solution.

6. Test for the presence of starch in each of the jars by dropping five drops of one solution onto the wax paper, adding two drops of iodine, and stirring with a toothpick. (A color of blue to blue-black is a positive test for starch.)

7. Record the resulting color.

8. Test each solution for the presence of glucose and starch every ten minutes for one hour.

Results

Iodine continues to turn the control solution blue-black; in the enzyme solution, the color changes from blue-black to amber. The Tes-Tape remains yellow for every test in the starch solution; in the enzyme solution, the tape progressively changes to a darker green.

Why?

Starch is a large **carbohydrate** (organic compound of carbon, hydrogen, and oxygen) molecule. Each starch molecule is made up of chains of a small sugar called **glucose.** This chainlike molecule is called a **polymer,** and the "links" in the chain are called **monomers.** Some starch molecules have more than a thousand links and thus form structures too large to pass through the small holes in the lining of the intestines.

Starch is our greatest source of food energy, but it must be broken into its separate links to be absorbed and used by the body. Digestive enzymes are protein **catalysts** that break up large starch molecules into smaller sugar molecules, called glucose. **Enzymes** are chemicals found in living cells that change the rate of reactions without themselves being chemically altered.

Try New Approaches

1. Is there a difference in the effectiveness of various manufacturers' processed food enzymes? Food enzymes purchased at a pharmacy are usually derived from a food-grain mold called *Aspergillus niger.* Determine their effectiveness by repeating the experiment using various brands of food enzymes.

2. How does the concentration of an enzyme affect its activity? Add 1 tablespoon (15 ml) of 1% starch solution to each of nine small jars (or test tubes). Number the jars from 0 to 8. The jar's number indicates the number of drops of enzyme that each container receives. Stir after the addition of each enzyme and test for the presence of iodine and glucose every ten minutes for one hour.

3. How does an acid pH affect enzymatic activity? Add 1 tablespoon (15 ml) of 1% starch solution and five drops of food enzyme to each of four small jars. Add 1 tablespoon (15 ml) of vinegar to one jar, 1 teaspoon (5 ml) of vinegar to the second jar, 1/3 teaspoon (1.7 ml) to the third jar, and no acid to the fourth jar. Stir the contents of each jar and test for the presence of iodine and glucose every ten minutes for one hour.

Design Your Own Experiment

1. Prepare a solution to test for the presence of glucose. Put a copper scrubbing pad in a jar. Cover the pad with household ammonia.

CAUTION: Ammonia is a poison. It and its fumes can damage skin and mucous membranes of nose, mouth, and eyes.

Allow the jar to stand until the solution is dark blue (about one day). In a small jar (or test tube), mix together 1 tablespoon (15 ml) of the blue test solution and 1 tablespoon (15 ml) of apple juice without added sugar. Set the jar in a saucepan of water (see Figure 27.2). Heat on a stove until the water in the saucepan boils and then let it boil for three minutes. The color indicates the glucose concentration present: blue (none), green (low concentration) yellow (modernate concentration), and orange to red (high concentration).

2. Design experiments to find the answers to the following questions:
   - How does an alkaline pH affect enzymatic activity?
   - Does the concentration of a **substrate** (substance on which an enzyme operates) affect the performance of the enzyme?

3. Fat molecules are very large and insoluble in water. To be transported in the blood, they must be changed into a form that will mix with water. One method of making fats mix with water is to emulsify them. An **emulsion** is a suspension of two **immiscible** liquids (liquids that do not mix together to form a solution), such as oil and water. When the small oil droplets are coated with an emulsifying agent, they remain suspended in the liquid and form a **colloid** (suspension that does not separate after standing).

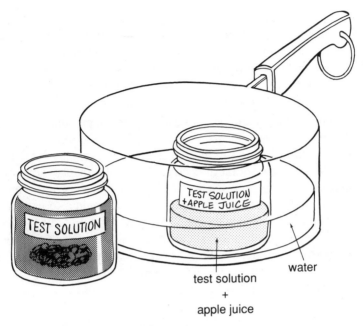

Figure 27.2

a. Use dishwashing liquid to demonstrate the effect of an emulsifying agent. Fill two small baby food jars three-fourths full with water. Add five drops of liquid cooking oil to each jar. Add five drops of dishwashing liquid to only one of the jars. Secure the lids on the jars and shake each one vigorously. Allow them to stand undisturbed for 5 to 10 minutes.

b. Much of the fat we eat is emulsified by the emulsifying agent called **bile,** which is secreted by the liver. Ask your teacher to order a 5% bile solution from a science supply company. Use this solution and repeat the experiment using bile instead of dishwashing liquid.

Get the Facts

1. Digestion breaks starch into smaller usable sugar molecules. What happens if too much starch is eaten? What does the body do with excess glucose that is produced?

2. What is the optimum pH for the most effective performance of stomach enzymes? Do intestinal enzymes function effectively in an acid or an alkaline environment?

3. Can humans digest the polysaccharide called *cellulose?* What is the difference between glycogen and cellulose? How can animals such as cows, rabbits, and termites digest the cellulose in the plants they eat? Cows and rabbits have large pouches in which food is stored while being digested. What are the names of these pouches? What part do they play in the digestive process of the organism?

4. Fat molecules are composed of carbon, hydrogen, and oxygen as are carbohydrate molecules. The ratio of hydrogen to oxygen in carbohydrates is 2:1; however, the ratio in fats is much greater. Find out more about the structure of fat molecules. You could display structural diagrams showing the four parts that make up fat molecules—a glycerol molecule and three fatty-acid molecules. You could also use structural diagrams to show the hydrolysis of fat. What is it about the fat molecule's structure that makes it the most concentrated energy reserve? What is the difference between saturated and unsaturated fat? How is a fat molecule changed to form a phospholipid? What is the importance of phospholipids?

28 Cellular Respiration

In mammals, energy is produced in the cells by the process of cellular respiration. Oxygen is taken into the red blood cells in the lungs, and carbon dioxide, the waste product of cellular respiration, is released from the blood into the lungs. The exchange rate of carbon dioxide and oxygen can be used to determine the rate of respiration in the body.

In this project, you will use indicators to test for the presence of carbon dioxide in exhaled breath. You will also study the effect of exercise and gender on respiration.

Getting Started

Purpose: To use an indicator to test for the presence of carbon dioxide in the exhaled breath.

Materials

2 small glass soda bottles

distilled water

marking pen

masking tape

brom thymol blue indicator
(see Appendix 2)

2 drinking straws

stopwatch

Procedure

1. Fill one soda bottle half full with distilled water. With the marking pen, write "Control" on a piece of masking tape and tape this label to the bottle.
2. Fill the second soda bottle half full with brom thymol blue indicator. Label the bottle "Brom Thymol Blue."
3. Use one straw to exhale into the brom thymol blue solution.

CAUTION: Be careful not to inhale any of the solution.

4. Start the stopwatch when you begin exhaling into the brom thymol blue. Stop the stopwatch when the solution turns yellow (see Figure 28.1).

177

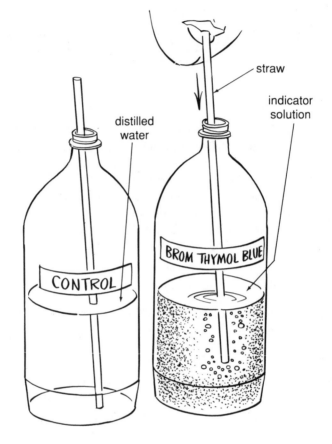

Figure 28.1

5. Record the total exhaling time.
6. Use the second (clean) straw to exhale into the distilled water.
7. Start the stopwatch when you begin exhaling into the water. Continue to exhale for a total time equal to that spent exhaling into the brom thymol blue solution.

Results

The time required to change the brom thymol blue solution from blue to yellow varies with each individual. There is no change in the color of the distilled water.

Why?

Brom thymol blue can be used to test for the presence of carbon dioxide gas. This indicator turns from blue to green and finally to yellow when mixed with different amounts of carbon dioxide. A two-step reaction occurs. First, carbon dioxide reacts with the water in the solution and produces carbonic acid. Then, this acid mixes with the brom thymol blue and causes its color to change from blue to yellow. The equations for the formation of carbonic acid is as follows:

$$CO_2 \quad + \quad H_2O \longrightarrow H_2CO_3$$

carbon dioxide plus *water* yields *carbonic acid*

Degrees of color changes of specific indicators as well as the rate at which they change give indications of the quantity of exhaled carbon dioxide and thus the rate of respiration.

Try New Approaches

1. Does exercise increase the carbon dioxide level in exhaled breath? Use brom thymol blue to compare the concentration of carbon dioxide in your breath before and after you exercise. The rate at which the indicator turns yellow can be used to compare the carbon dioxide concentrations. The stronger the acid concentration, the faster the color change and the greater the degree of yellow coloring. A strong acidic solution is an indication of a high level of carbon dioxide in each exhaled breath. For best results, check the carbon dioxide content of several people before and after they exercise. Be sure that they do equivalent amounts of exercise and choose an exercise that each person can do without endangering his or her health.

2. Limewater can be used to test for the presence of carbonic acid. Repeat the original and preceding experiments substituting limewater (see Appendix 2) for brom thymol blue. Use a second bottle of limewater for a color comparison.

   Limewater, the common name for a calcium hydroxide solution, is used to test for the presence of carbon dioxide gas. This indicator turns cloudy in the presence of a carbonic acid solution, and forms calcium carbonate, a white, chalky, insoluble solid. It is the formation of the calcium carbonate that turns the solution cloudy. The equation for this reaction is as follows:

$$Ca(OH)_2 \quad + \quad H_2CO_3 \quad \longrightarrow CaCO_3 \quad + \quad 2H_2O$$

calcium plus *carbonic* yields *calcium* plus *water*

hydroxide   *acid*   *carbonate*

3. Red cabbage extract can be used to test for the presence of carbonic acid. This indicator turns from purple to red in the presence of an acid. Repeat the original experiment substituting red cabbage extract (see Appendix 2) for brom thymol blue. Use a second bottle of red cabbage extract for color comparison. The more carbon dioxide dissolved in the liquid, the stronger the acid and the greater the degree of red coloring. The rate of the color change also increases with larger amounts of dissolved carbon dioxide.

4. Does gender affect the amount of carbon dioxide exhaled? Repeat the original experiment three times testing an equal number of males and females each time: First, use brom thymol blue as the carbon dioxide indicator; second, replace the brom thymol blue indicator with limewater; and third, replace the brom thymol blue with red cabbage extract. Compare the results from all three tests. **Science Fair Hint:** Use photographs to represent the procedure of each experiment. Display colored diagrams of each container of indicator before and after the addition of carbon dioxide.

Design Your Own Experiment

Note: Only take on the following project if you or someone else you know is willing to keep and maintain the fish after the experiment.

1. Do aquatic organisms undergo cellular respiration? Use one goldfish of medium size to test for the presence of carbon dioxide in its water. Fill two clean 1-quart (1-liter) jars with distilled water. Label the jars "Control," and 1. Allow the water to stand until it reaches room temperature before placing one fish into jar 1 (see Figure 28.2). Cover each jar with a clean cloth and place the jars in an area of little or no activity in order to encourage the fish to be more restful. After 24 hours, carefully remove the fish from the jar. *Note:* The fish will be used again, but will be returned to the aquarium until needed.

Use steps 1, 2, and 3 in Appendix 2 to make two separate brom thymol blue solutions using the water in the two jars. Observe and record the color of the solution in each jar. The control jar should be

distilled water

Figure 28.2

blue. The presence of carbon dioxide changes the blue color to green or yellow; green indicates a lower carbon dioxide level; yellow a higher level. Display photographs of the jars containing the fish and samples of the brom thymol solutions.

2. How does increased activity affect the results of this experiment? After 24 hours, repeat the preceding experiment using the same fish used previously. Place the uncovered jars in an area of constant activity. Approach and touch (not tapping) the jar containing the fish often during the test period to increase the activity of the fish. Use a color chart to compare the results of the activity with the less-active fish.

Get the Facts

1. Use a biology text to find out the percentage of carbon dioxide in your exhaled breath while at rest and during exercise. You could make and display a pie chart to represent this information.
2. The rate of respiration is directly related to the breathing rate. Rapid, deep breathing results in an increase in the respiration rate. Find out more about how breathing rate is controlled. When cells need more

oxygen, there is an increase in the rate and depth of breathing. What triggers this response? How does the portion of the brain called the *medulla oblongata* regulate the carbon dioxide content of the blood?

3. Aerobic respiration requires oxygen. *Aerobic* means that something lives or occurs in the presence of air. Find out more about the respiration reaction. What is the difference between aerobic and anaerobic respiration? Which produces the most energy? Write and display chemical equations to represent these energy-producing reactions. Write the equation showing the anaerobic respiration in muscle cells due to excessive exercise. In aerobic respiration, what is the ATP–ADP cycle? Use a diagram to represent this series of chemical events.

29 Operant Conditioning: "Aha!" Respons

When confronted with alternatives, animals with bilaterally symmetrical nervous systems can learn to make consistent choices. Sometimes, learning is a response to a particular stimulus or to a reward. Other times, learning comes through force of habit, or trial and error, or insight.

In this project, you will study the human ability to learn by trial and error as well as through insight. The ability of mice and insects to learn as a result of operant conditioning—that is, to learn as a result of receiving rewards for desired behavior—will be determined. You will also look at factors that may affect the retention and rate of learning, such as practice and distractions.

Getting Started

Purpose: To determine the time it takes for a person to trace the mirror image of a pattern.

Materials

20-x-24-x-36-inch (50-x-61-x-90-cm) cardboard box

box cutter

24-x-16-inch (60-x-40-cm) mirror

duct tape

felt-tip marking pen

10 copies of test sheet (Draw your own. See Figure 29.1)

10 test subjects

timer

Procedure

1. Build a mirror test box (see Figure 29.1). *Note:* The size of the box and mirror are not critical. You want a box and mirror large enough to allow each test subject to see only the mirror image of the pattern and be able to insert his or her hand without restriction to trace the pattern. Here are the steps followed by the author in building a test box using the listed materials.

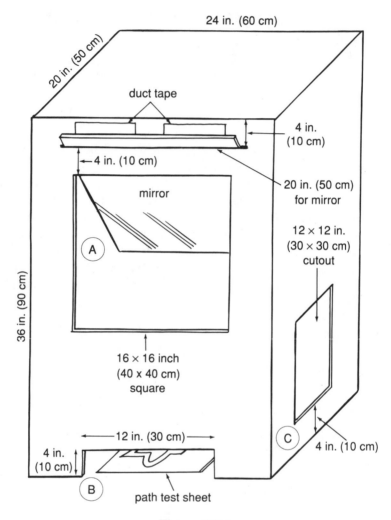

24 in. (60 cm)

20 in. (50 cm)

duct tape

4 in. (10 cm)

4 in. (10 cm)

mirror

20 in. (50 cm) for mirror

12 × 12 in. (30 × 30 cm) cutout

A

36 in. (90 cm)

16 × 16 inch (40 x 40 cm) square

12 in. (30 cm)

4 in. (10 cm)

C

4 in. (10 cm)

B

path test sheet

Figure 29.1

a. In the front wall of the box, 4 inches (10 cm) down from the top, use the box cutter to cut a 20-inch (50-cm) slit across the center of the box.

b. In the back wall of the box, 17 inches (43 cm) down from the top, cut a 20-inch (50 cm) slit across the center of the box.

c. Insert the edges of the mirror (face down) through the slits in the front and back walls of the box.

    d. Use duct tape to secure the edges of the mirror to the box.

    e. Cut a 16-x-16-inch (40-x-40-cm) square out of the front wall of the box. Make sure this hole is centered and its top edge is about 4 inches (10 cm) below the edge of the mirror (see A in Figure 29.1).

    f. Cut a 4-x-12-inch (10-x-30-cm) section from the bottom edge of the front wall of the box (see B in Figure 29.1).

    g. To allow viewing light to enter, cut out one 12-inch (30-cm) square from each side of the box with the lower edge of the square about 4 inches (10 cm) from the bottom of the box (see C in Figure 29.1).

2. Set the mirror test box on a table.

3. Lay the marking pen and one copy of the test sheet inside the box. (see Figure 29.2)

4. Have the test subject sit in a chair positioned in front of the test box.

5. Read the following instructions to one test subject:

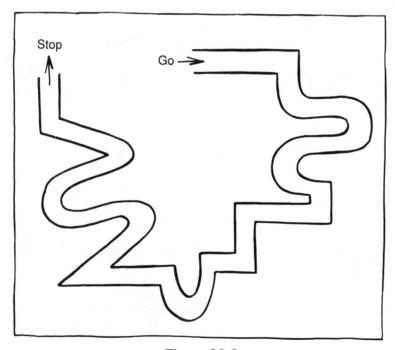

Figure 29.2

- Follow the instructions as I read them to you.
- Insert your hand through the opening at the bottom of the box.
- Look at the mirror through the opening in the center of the box.
- The objective is for you to use the pen to draw a line though the center of the path on the test sheet as fast as possible without crossing the printed lines of the pattern. When I say "Get ready . . . Start," you will begin and I will start the timer. When you finish, say "Stop" and the timer will be stopped.
- Place the tip of the pen on the word "Go" on the sheet.
- Get ready.
- Start.

6. Repeat the procedure for all of the test subjects.

Results

The time varies for each person tested.

Why?

The test subjects learn to trace the pattern of the mirror image of the path by a method called **insight response** or the **"aha!" response**. Insight responses are entirely new responses but depend upon previously learned responses put together in a new way. The faster the test subject learns to compensate for the fact that the up and down movements in the mirror image are backward, the faster is his or her time for completing the path.

Try New Approaches

1. Can the test subjects improve their time with practice? To determine whether the amount of practice time affects the results, assign each person a different number of practices—from one to ten, respectively. Allow the subjects to practice and then repeat the experiment. **Science Fair Hint:** Prepare a learning curve for each subject. Use the y-axis for the time per path and the x-axis for the number of practices (see Figure 29.3).

2. Do distractions affect the tracing time? Repeat the original experiment using ten different test subjects. During the timing period, provide the same distractions for each subject, such as playing a radio and/or having someone talk to the person being timed.

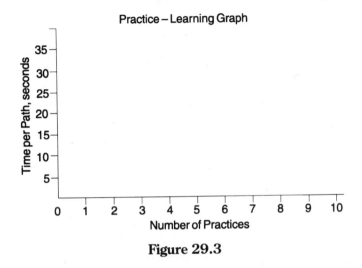

Figure 29.3

3. How does spacing the practice period affect the time of the learner? Use a different set of test subjects. Allow all subjects to practice for the same amount of time. Have half of the subjects do all their practice in one session and the other half practice over several days. After the practice sessions, repeat the original experiment.

Design Your Own Experiment

1. Are the test subjects faster at solving mazes that are not mirror images? Without the use of the mirror test box, determine the time required for each subject to draw a path through a maze designed by you and printed on a sheet of paper. Provide ten copies of the maze and record the time for each person to complete each maze in succession. Graph the results.

2. The method of using rewards to train an animal to perform tasks that are not **innate** (inborn) is known as **instrumental conditioning** or **operant conditioning**. By operant conditioning, ants and mice can be trained to solve mazes. They will find their way through a maze in order to find food. After they have gone through the maze once, the speed of solving the maze increases with each subsequent test. Design and construct mazes for these organisms to solve. Determine the number of errors per trial. Graph the trials on the x-axis and the errors on the y-axis. Display as many of the test materials as possible without

overcrowding the display area. Use photographs of the subjects during testing.

Get the Facts

1. The movements required to trace the mirror image of the path involve brain activity. Muscular movements are controlled by the parts of the brain called the *cerebellum* and *cerebrum*. Find out more about the cerebellum and cerebrum. In which do impulses resulting in muscle movement originate? Where are the impulses coordinated?

2. Insight responses are very creative acts and involve *inductive* and *deductive reasoning*. Find out about these two types of learning processes. Which type of reasoning involves learning the general principle that mirror images are upside down? Down is up? Up is down? Applying the knowledge that the directions are reversed involves which of the processes?

3. Training by offering a reward for a specific activity is called *instrumental* or *operant conditioning*. The psychologist B. F. Skinner used this method to train pigeons to play Ping-Pong. Use a psychology or biology text dealing with learned behavior to find out more about the training of animals to perform tasks that are not innate.

30 | Effect of Stimuli on Reaction Times

A basketball rolls across the street in front of a moving car. The driver must make split-second decisions about what to do. The driver's reaction time, how long it takes for the person to respond, involves special sensory and motor nerve cells that send and receive messages to and from the brain.

In this project, you will compare reaction times to a visual stimulus and reaction times to an auditory stimulus. You will also explore whether other factors, such as distraction, gender, and age, affect reaction time.

Getting Started

Purpose: To determine your reaction time to a visual stimulus.

Material

table and chair   yardstick (meterstick)

helper

Procedure

1. Sit with your forearm on the surface of the table with your writing hand extending over the edge.

2. Have your helper position the yardstick (meterstick) with the zero end between, but not touching, your thumb and fingers (see Figure 30.1).

3. Instruct your helper to release the stick without warning.

4. As soon as the stick is released, try to catch it as quickly as possible between your thumb and fingers.

5. Record the distance the stick falls and use the following equation to determine your reaction time. See Appendix 5 for a sample calculation.

$$Time = \sqrt{\frac{2 \times distance\ the\ stick\ falls}{386\ inches\ (980cm)\ per\ second\ squared}}$$

6. Record the distance and time calculated for the one trial.

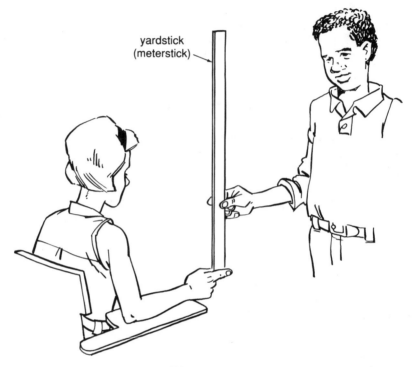

yardstick
(meterstick)

Figure 30.1

Results

The reaction time varies with each individual.

Why?

Your eye is the **stimulus receptor** that sees the stick as it starts to fall. It detects the movement of the stick and initiates a signal, a nerve impulse, in the nerve cell to which it is attached. The message is then sent along **sensory neurons** (special nerve cells that transmit impulses from the stimulus receptor) to the spinal cord. The spinal cord telegraphs the message to the brain, where it is processed. A message is transmitted from the brain down the spinal cord to **motor neurons,** which cause the muscles in your hand to contract so that your fingers clamp around the falling stick. The time for these impulses to make the complete trip from the stimulus receptor to the motor neurons is called the **reaction time.**

Try New Approaches

1. Does practice affect reaction time? Repeat the experiment 10 times. Calculate your reaction time for each trial and plot the data on a graph. Study the graph to determine whether the trend of repeated trials is toward faster or slower reaction times. Explain what accounts for the results.

2. Does using your writing hand affect reaction time? Use your other hand and repeat the procedure in the original experiment 10 times. Graph the data and compare the results for both hands.

3. Is reaction time affected if you are distracted? Have a second helper ask you simple math problems as you repeat the procedure in the original experiment 10 times.

4. How does using an auditory stimulus receptor affect reaction time? Repeat the procedure in the original experiment, but this time close your eyes. Have your helper say "Go" when he or she releases the stick. Try to react to the auditory stimulus as quickly as possible by catching the stick. Calculate your reaction times for 10 trials and graph them (see Figure 30.2). The time delay between the helper's releasing his or her fingers and saying "Go" is very slight, but you might want to design an experiment that eliminates this delay. One idea would be to have the stick support a lever attached to a bell. When the stick is released the bell rings, notifying you that the stick is falling.

5. Does age affect reaction time? Repeat the procedure in the original experiment using a test group of people in good health and of the same gender but of different ages. Test each person 10 times and average the results. Plot the averages on a graph.

6. Does gender affect reaction time? Repeat the procedure in the previous experiment using an equal number of males and females, all of whom are in good health and of the same age. Test each person ten times and average the results. Plot the averages on a graph.

Design Your Own Experiment

1a. Use a test group to collect more data on reaction time. Draw a 1-foot (30-cm) square in the center of a piece of cardboard. Divide the square into sixteen even parts. Randomly write the numbers 1 through 16 in the squares. The objective is for the person being tested to touch the numbers in numerical order. As each number is

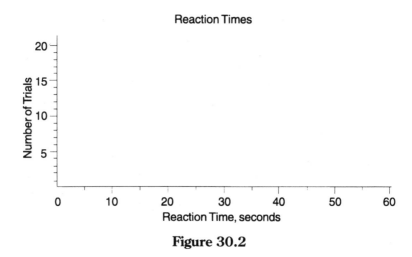

Figure 30.2

touched, have the person call that number aloud. Record the time for all 16 squares to be touched.

b. Determine whether practice improves reaction time by having each person in the test group repeat the activity ten times.

c. Test the effect of distractions on reaction time by asking each person questions during the activity.

d. Average the results of each activity and record the averages on a bar graph.

2. How does fatigue affect reaction time? Is there any variation in reaction time after physical fatigue or mental fatigue? Design an experiment that tests these factors.

Get the Facts

1. How do factors such as diet, alcohol, tobacco, or other drugs affect the ability of a person to react to a stimulus? Use the library and/or a medical physician or psychiatrist as sources of information for a report that explains the effects of these factors on reaction time. A nerve impulse is an electrical impulse that flows at a rate of about 133 yards (122 m) per second. Do drugs affect the speed of nerve impulses?

2. How does practice improve the reaction time for a specific activity? Discover whether any changes are made in the brain by practicing an activity.

3. How are muscle movements controlled? Find out more about muscle control. Describe the path of the impulses from the time the eye receives the message that the yardstick (meterstick) is released to the moment the muscles in the hands contract around the stick. You could draw a diagram to represent this path.

4. Muscles contract and relax due to nerve impulses. What is the direct cause of the contraction? List and describe the effect of chemicals that are naturally found in the body and that are involved in this muscle movement.

Appendix 1

Microscopic Slide Preparation

Wet mounts used to view some specimens with a microscope. A wet mount is just a drop of water and an object to be studied on a slide covered with a coverslip. Use the following procedure to prepare a wet mount.

1. Place a clean slide on a table.
2. Place the specimen to be studied on the slide.
3. Use an eyedropper to place one drop of water on the specimen (see Figure A1.1).
4. Hold the coverslip so that one side just touches the edge of the drop of water (see Figure A1.2). Let the coverslip drop. Good slides have few air bubbles trapped under the coverslip, so make a new slide if too many bubbles are present.

Figure A1.1

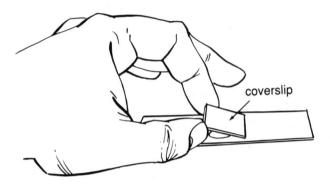

Figure A1.2

Appendix 2

Preparing Solutions and Reagents

Brom Thymol Blue

Materials

1-quart (1-liter) jar with lid

1 quart (1 liter) of distilled water

0.035 ounces (0.1g) brom thymol blue

eyedropper (if necessary)

household ammonia (if necessary)

Procedure

1. Fill the jar with distilled water.
2. Add the brom thymol blue to the jar.
3. Secure the lid and shake the jar to mix.
4. If the solution appears green or yellow, add one drop of household ammonia, one drop at a time, until the solution appears blue.

Limewater (Calcium Hydroxide)

Materials

2 1-quart (1-liter) glass jars with lids

distilled water

teaspoon (5 ml)

calcium oxide (lime used in making pickles)

marking pen

masking tape

Procedure

1. Fill one jar with distilled water.
2. Add 1 teaspoon (5 ml) of lime and stir.
3. Secure the lid. Allow the solution to stand overnight.
4. Decant (pour off) the clear liquid into the second jar. *Note:* Be careful

not to pour any of the lime that has settled on the bottom of the jar.

5. Secure the lid and keep the jar closed.

6. With the marking pen, write "Limewater" on a piece of masking tape and tape this label to the jar.

Red Cabbage Extract

Materials

small head of red cabbage	tea strainer
2-quart (2-liter) cooking pot	1-quart (1-liter) jar with lid
distilled water	refrigerator
stove	

Procedure

1. Tear the cabbage leaves into small pieces and place them into the cooking pot.

2. Fill the pot with distilled water.

3. Heat on the stove to boiling and boil the liquid for five minutes.

4. Allow the liquid to cool.

5. Pour the cooled cabbage extract through the tea strainer into the jar. Discard the cabbage leaves.

6. Store the concentrated cabbage extract in the refrigerator until needed.

7. When ready to use, mix equal parts of the concentrated cabbage extract and distilled water.

Starch Solution (1%)

Materials

½ teaspoon (2.5 ml) of cornstarch	small saucepan
	stove
1 cup (250 ml) of distilled water	1-pint (500-ml) jar with lid

Procedure

1. Mix the cornstarch with 1 tablespoon (15 ml) of distilled water to form a paste.

2. Pour the remaining water into the saucepan and heat on the stove to boiling.

3. Slowly add the starch paste.

4. Cook for two minutes, stirring constantly.

5. Allow the solution to cool.

6. Pour the solution into the jar and secure the lid.

Appendix 3

Random Sampling in an Open Ecosystem

Use the following procedure to calculate the abundance of plant life in each sampling area.

1. Count the number of each plant type.
2. Determine the total number of all plants.
3. Determine the abundance of each plant type as a percentage of the total number of all the plants.

Example
If there are 30 woody plants and 300 total plants in a sampling area, the abundance of woody plants is calculated as follows:

$$\text{abundance} = \frac{30 \text{ woody plants}}{300 \text{ total plants}} \times 100\% = \textbf{10\% woody plants}$$

Use the following procedure to calculate the density of plant life in each sampling area.

1. Count the number of each plant type.
2. Determine the area of the sampling plot.
3. Divide the total number of each plant type by the area of the sampling plot.

Example
If there are ten trees in a 100-square-yard (100-square-meter) area, the density of trees is calculated as follows:

$$\text{density} = \frac{10 \text{ trees}}{100 \text{ yd}^2 \text{ (m}^2\text{)}} = \textbf{0.1 tree/yd}^2 \textbf{ (m}^2\textbf{)}$$

Use the following procedure to calculate the frequency of each plant type.

1. Determine how many of the subplots have each type of plant.

2. Determine the frequency by dividing the number of subplots with a specific plant type by the total number of subplots, which is 9 for the projects in this book.

Example

If six subplots have trees, the frequency of trees in the total test plot is calculated as follows:

$$\text{frequency} = \frac{6}{9} \times 100\% = \textbf{67\%}$$

Appendix 4

Preserving Plants

Pressing Leaves and Plants

Materials

8 to 10 sheets of newspaper

2 sheets of white construction paper

leaves or small plants

5 heavy books

Procedure

1. Place four or five sheets of newspaper on a table where they will not be disturbed.
2. Lay one sheet of construction paper in the center of the newspaper sheets.
3. Arrange the leaves on the construction paper with their veiny sides down. (see Figure A4.1). *Note:* Small plants with thin stems and roots can be arranged on the paper.
4. Place the second sheet of construction paper on top of the leaves or plants.
5. Cover the construction paper with four or five sheets of newspaper to help absorb moisture from the leaves or plants.
6. Stack five heavy books on top of the papers, making sure the books are centered over the leaves or plants.
7. After two weeks, remove the books and uncover the flat, dried leaves or plants. *Note:* For display purposes, label each leaf or plant and place the sheet of construction paper with the arranged leaves or plants in a picture frame. Or, use rubber cement to glue the leaves to construction paper and label each leaf.

Leaf Prints

Materials

3 or 4 sheets of newspaper

2 sheets of typing paper

leaves

crayon

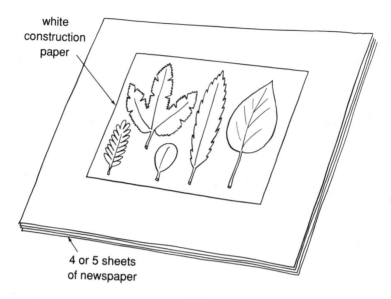

white
construction
paper

4 or 5 sheets
of newspaper

Figure A4.1

Procedure

1. Place three or four sheets of newspaper on a table to protect the table's surface.

2. Lay one sheet of typing paper on top of the newspaper sheets.

3. Arrange the leaves on the typing paper with their rough, veiny sides up.

4. Cover the leaves with the second sheet of typing paper.

5. With firm pressure, rub the crayon across the paper over the area of the leaves so that a colored imprint of each leaf is formed (see Figure A4.2).

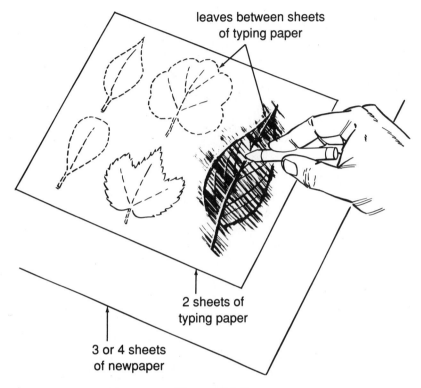

leaves between sheets
of typing paper

2 sheets of
typing paper

3 or 4 sheets
of newpaper

Figure A4.2

Appendix 5

Calculating Falling Rate

Example
If a yardstick (meterstick) falls 18 inches (45.7 cm) through a person's fingers before being caught, the reaction time of the person is calculated as follows:

distance the stick falls = 18 inches (45.7 cm)

gravitational acceleration = 386 inches (980 cm) per second squared (s²)

$$\text{time} = \sqrt{\frac{2 \times \text{distance the stick falls}}{\text{gravitational acceleration}}}$$

$$= \sqrt{\frac{2 \times 18 \text{ inches}}{386 \text{ inches/s}^2}} = \sqrt{\frac{2 \times 45.7 \text{ cm}}{980 \text{cm/s}^2}}$$

$$= 0.31 \text{ second} \quad = 0.31 \text{ second}$$

Glossary

abiotic factors   The physical aspects of an environment; temperature, erosion, slope of the land.

adhesion   Molecular attraction between dissimilar molecules; attraction between water molecules and molecules that make up the inside of a xylem tube.

adventitious roots   Roots that develop directly from stems or leaves instead of from the normal root system.

aerobic   In the presence of oxygen.

"aha!" response   See *insight response.*

amylase   Enzyme that is found in saliva and that begins the digestion of starch molecules in the mouth.

anaerobic   Without the presence of oxygen.

angiosperms   Flowering plants.

apical   Being at or near the tip or apex.

apical dominance   Inhibition of growth of lateral buds on a stem by the growth of the apical (terminal) shoot.

aquaponics   The growing of plants in a 100% liquid nutrient solution without the aid of a supporting medium.

asexual reproduction   Method of reproducing a new organism from only one parent by means of mitosis.

auxin   Hormone that causes the cells in a plant to lengthen. A positive response to auxin is the growth of cells; a negative response is the inhibition of growth.

bacteria   Very small, one-celled, microscopic organisms found in air, water, soil, and the bodies of other living organisms; bacterium, singular form.

bactericidal   Able to kill bacteria.

biotic factors   Relationships among organisms.

bolus   Rounded mass; wet ball of food pushed through the esophagus.

calcium propionate   Food additive that inhibits mold growth in foods.

capillary action   The rising of a liquid in a small tube because of adhesive and cohesive forces.

carbohydrate   Organic compound containing carbon, hydrogen, and oxygen. The hydrogen-to-oxygen ratio is 2:1.

cast   Undigested soil deposited at the surface of the soil by earthworms.

catalyst   Chemical that changes the rate of a chemical reaction without itself being chemically altered.

chlorophyll   Green plant pigment that is found in chloroplasts and is necessary for photosynthesis.

chloroplasts   Plant cell structures containing light-sensitive chlorophyll.

cohesion   Attraction between similar molecules; attraction between two water molecules.

coleoptile   Protective sheath that encloses the primary leaf of young grass plants and other germinating monocots.

colloid   Suspension that does not separate on standing.

colony   Group of bacteria cells.

complemental air   Amount of air that can be forcefully inhaled.

cotyledon   Seed leaf that stores food for a plant embryo of seed plants.

culture medium   Specially prepared nutritious substance used to grow experimental organisms.

dehydrate   Lose water.

dicot   Plant that has seeds with two seed leaves.

dicotyledon   Flowering plant with two cotyledons; beans; called a *dicot.*

disaccharide   Sugar formed by the combination of two simple sugar molecules.

ecological community   Ecosystem.

ecosystem   Interaction of living organisms with their environment.

egg   First stage in the metamorphosis of some insects; female sex cell.

embryo   Early development of an animal or a plant after fertilization; cylindrical structure within a seed that develops into a plant.

emulsion   Suspension of two immiscible liquids.

enzyme   Protein catalyst; chemical that changes the rate of a chemical reaction in living tissue without itself being chemically altered.

epicotyl   End of a plant embryo that develops into the plant's first true leaves.

etiolation   Elongation of plant cells caused by lack of sunlight.

expiration   Process of breathing out.

fermentation   Release of energy from sugar without the use of oxygen; anaerobic respiration.

filtrate   Liquid that passes through the pores in a filter.

fragmentation   Example of asexual reproduction. A new plant grows from a part broken from a parent plant.

geoponic   Grown in the earth.

geotropism   Growth response of plants to gravity. Stems grow upward and roots grow downward.

germinate   Develop from a seed into a plant.

glucose   One of the simplest and most important sugars. Serves as the basic transportable form of fuel for living organisms.

GRAS list   List of food additives that are considered "Generally Recognized As Safe."

gymnosperms   Evergreens or conifers.

hilum   Scar on a bean that marks the spot where the seed was attached to the ovary wall.

homeostasis   Ability of a cell to regulate a stable internal environment by controlling the passage of fluids into and out of the cell.

hydroponics   The growing of plants in a liquid nutrient solution.

hydroponicum   Hydroponic growing unit.

hypertonic solution   Solution having a lower water concentration than a solution to which it is compared.

hyperventilation   Extravigorous breathing.

hypocotyl   Part of the embryo inside a seed that develops into the plant's lower stem and roots.

hypotonic solution   Solution having a higher water concentration than a solution to which it is compared.

immiscible   Incapable of mixing together to form a solution.

innate   Inborn; not acquired by experience or instruction.

inoculation   Introduction of a sample of material into a prepared container; placement of bacteria onto a culture medium.

insight response   New response to a situation that depends upon previously learned responses.

inspiration   Process of breathing in.

instrumental conditioning   See *operant conditioning.*

larva   Second stage in the metamorphosis of some insects; commonly called a *maggot.*

lateral growth   Growth from the side; side branches or shoots on a plant stem.

leaching   Process of removing the soluble chemicals from soil. Water is filtered through the soil and water-soluble chemicals are extracted.

maltose   A disaccharide or double sugar made of two glucose molecules.

meristem   Part of a plant that carries on cell division resulting in growth; from the Greek word *meristos,* which means "divided."

metamorphosis   Series of changes that take place as an egg develops into an adult, including the four stages of egg, larva, pupa, and adult.

micropyle   Small opening at the end of the hilum through which pollen grains enter.

mitosis   Process of cell duplication, in which two daughter cells receive exactly the same nuclear material as the original cell.

monocotyledon   A seed plant with one cotyledon; corn; called a *monocot.*

monomers Single molecules linked together to form a polymer.

motor neurons Special nerve cells that transmit impulses to the muscles.

nutrient Nourishment; food that promotes growth in living organisms.

operant conditioning Method of using rewards to train an animal to perform tasks that are not innate.

operculum Protective flap of skin over a fish's gills.

osmosis Movement of water through a semipermeable membrane from an area of greater water concentration to an area of lesser water concentration.

osmotic pressure Force produced by the pressure of water diffusing through a semipermeable membrane. The greater the difference in water concentration on either side of the membrane, the greater the osmotic pressure.

peristalsis Wavelike contractions of muscles in tubular organs; motion that forces food through the human digestive organs; means of locomotion in earthworms.

phloem Tubes used to transport food manufactured in the leaves of plants to other parts of the plant.

photomorphogenesis Plant responses to light stimuli that are not specifically directional or periodic.

photoperiodism Development of an organism depending on the duration of daylight or darkness.

photosynthesis Energy-making reaction in plants; formation of carbohydrates in chlorophyll-containing tissue of plants exposed to light. Carbon dioxide, water, and sunlight are used to produce oxygen, sugar, and energy.

phototropism Growth response of plants to light.

plastids Organelles formed from proplastids that usually contain pigment, but some are colorless.

polymer A large molecule formed by many small molecules linked together in chainlike fashion.

proplastid A colorless structure in cells from which plastids originate.

pupa Third stage in the metamorphosis of some insects.

radicle Tip of the hypocotyl inside a seed which develops into the plant's first root.

reaction time Time it takes a nerve impulse to travel from a sensory receptor to the motor neurons; time to see a falling object and clamp the hand shut in order to catch it.

reserve air Amount of air that can be forced out of the lungs after normal expiration.

residual air Amount of air left in the lungs after forced expiration.

respiration   Reaction in the cells of plants and animals that uses oxygen and sugar to produce carbon dioxide, water, and energy.

scientific method   A series of logically related steps used to gather information in order to solve a problem.

seed coat   Protective covering around a seed.

semipermeable membrane   Membrane that selectively allows materials to pass through.

sensory neurons   Special nerve cells that transmit impulses from a stimulus receptor.

stereomicroscope   Microscope that provides less magnification than most microscopes and that is used to view large organisms or objects; called a *dissecting microscope.*

stimulus receptors   Sensory organs that respond to stimuli; organs that respond to sight, sound, smell, touch, and taste.

stomata   Special openings in the epidermis of a leaf through which gases pass.

substrate   Substance on which an enzyme operates.

terminal   At the end; apical.

tidal air   Amount of air involved during normal breathing.

translocation   Movement of water, minerals, and food through the plant.

transpiration   Evaporation of water through pores in the leaves of plants called *stomata.*

tropism   Movement of plants in response to stimuli.

turgor pressure   Pressure inside a cell caused by the presence of water.

vascular plants   Plants that have vascular tissues for transporting food, minerals, and water.

vegetative propagation   Reproduction from a nonsexual part of an organism; asexual reproduction; new plants grown from a cutting taken from a plant.

ventrally   In the front, near the bottom.

vital capacity   Maximum volume of air inhaled or exhaled during forced breathing.

xylem vessels   Thick-walled, cylindrical tubes that transport water and nutrients from a plant's roots to other parts of the plant.

Index

Get these fun and exciting books by Janice VanCleave
at your local bookstore, call toll-free 1-800-225-5945, or fill out the order form below and mail to:
Molly Chesney, John Wiley & Sons, Inc., 605 Third Ave., NY, NY 10158

Janice VanCleave's Science For Every Kid Series

___Astronomy	53573-7	$11.95 US / 15.95 CAN
___Biology	50381-9	$11.95 US / 15.95 CAN
___Chemistry	62085-8	$11.95 US / 15.95 CAN
___Dinosaurs	30812-9	$11.95 US / 15.95 CAN
___Earth Science	53010-7	$11.95 US / 15.95 CAN
___Ecology	10086-2	$11.95 US / 15.95 CAN
___Geography	59842-9	$11.95 US / 15.95 CAN
___Geometry	31141-3	$11.95 US / 15.95 CAN
___Human Body	02408-2	$11.95 US / 15.95 CAN
___Math	54265-2	$11.95 US / 15.95 CAN
___Oceans	12453-2	$11.95 US / 15.95 CAN
___Physics	52505-7	$11.95 US / 15.95 CAN

Janice VanCleave's Spectacular Science Projects

___Animals	55052-3	$10.95 US / 12.95 CAN
___Earthquakes	57107-5	$10.95 US / 12.95 CAN
___Electricity	31010-7	$10.95 US / 12.95 CAN
___Gravity	55050-7	$10.95 US / 12.95 CAN
___Machines	57108-3	$10.95 US / 12.95 CAN
___Magnets	57106-7	$10.95 US / 12.95 CAN
___Microscopes & Magnifying Lenses	58956-X	$10.95 US / 12.95 CAN
___Molecules	55054-X	$10.95 US / 12.95 CAN
___Rocks and Minerals	10269-5	$10.95 US / 12.95 CAN
___Volcanoes	30811-0	$10.95 US / 12.95 CAN
___Weather	03231-X	$10.95 US / 12.95 CAN

Janice VanCleave's Science Bonanzas

___200 Gooey, Slippery, Slimy, Weird & Fun Experiments	57921-1	$12.95 US / 16.95 CAN
___201 Awesome, Magical, Bizarre & Incredible Experiments	31011-5	$12.95 US / 16.95 CAN
___202 Oozing, Bubbling, Dripping & Bouncing Experiments	14025-2	$12.95 US / 16.95 CAN

Janice VanCleave's A+ Projects

___Biology	58628-5	$12.95 US / 17.95 CAN
___Chemistry	58630-7	$12.95 US / 17.95 CAN

[ ] Check/Money order enclosed
(Wiley pays shipping. Please include $2.50 for handling charges.)
[ ] Charge my: [ ]VISA [ ]MASTERCARD [ ]AMEX [ ]DISCOVER
Card #:_____ Expiration Date:_____/_____
NAME:_____
ADDRESS:_____
CITY/STATE/ZIP:_____
SIGNATURE:_____

(Order not valid unless signed)

WILEY
Publishers Since 1807